Black, Gray and White

The Transformation of Her Heart

By Megas Adelphos

New Life Clarity Publishing
205 West 300 South, Brigham City, Utah 84302
Http://newlifeclarity.com/

The Right of Ron Britton to be identified as the author of the work has been asserted by him in accordancewith the Copyright Act 1988.

New Life Clarity Publishing
name has been established by NLCP CORP.

All Rights Reserved.
No part of this publication may be reproduced, distributed, or transmitted in any form or by any means, including photocopying, recording, or other electronic or mechanical methods without the prior and express written permission of the author or publisher, except in the case of brief quotations embodied in critical reviews and certain other noncommercial uses permitted by copyright law.

Printed in the United States of America

ISBN- 9781088026335

Copyright@2023 Ron Britton

Introduction

Black and white mixed together turns into the color grey. There are many grey areas when it comes to relationships. This will be part of a series called, "The Modern-Day Songs of Solomon." The Songs of Solomon discusses in depth difficulties and ins and outs of relationships both on a natural and spiritual level.

I created these writings out of my own life experiences of being unsuccessful and successful in encounters with relationships. This is the second book of the series I will complete.

My hope is that the series will be a healing balm for those who did not have any success with finding a great relationship, their life partner or soul mate. There is a transformation process that takes place in the heart of a woman when she is fully content with a man that loves her unconditionally.

A woman's eyes change colors from the myriad of emotions she feels. May love rule as the catalyst for change in relationships.

About The Author

I am a P.A.L. (poet, author, and lyricist) and I have been writing for over 22 years. Black, Gray, and White is a modern-day version of the "Songs of Solomon. Solomon was a prolific writer in every respect of being one of the greatest writers ever to pen poetry and songs. I have been a case manager for over 15 years in which I have combined both my deep talent for writing poetry and mixing it up with my experiences as a mental health case manager. I work at two of the most influential organizations on the West Coast that provides services for youth and adults.

Black, Gray and White is part of a trio serial called "Noveltry". This book will be the second in the series. I hope to stir intriguing interest of the poet readers by giving them some suspense and some thought-provoking memories of their own experiences. This is the first of a kind style of writing in which hope will mesmerize the hearts of many.

In relationships, there are many twists and turns and we are the product and outcome of what we have invested or not invested. May this book be an enlightenment of what can be or not to be. It is black, gray, or white.

TABLE OF CONTENTS

Introduction..iii
About The Author..v

1. Poisonous Ways..1
2. Another Man's Hands..3
3. Little Girl..5
4. So Many Hands..7
5. Black Widow..8
6. And I Reached...9
7. Almond Shape..10
8. At the Altar..11
9. A Love I have almost had...13
10. Beautiful in Red...15
11. Before God..16
12. Before We Sleep..17
13. Betrayal...18
14. Black Rose...19
15. **Black** Spice..20
16. Come Here..21
17. Yellow Dress..23
18. Shades of Orange..25
19. Pale Flower..26
20. Love in Purple...27

Table of Contents

21.	Love and War	29
22.	Blue Crystal	31
23.	Beyond My Color	33
24.	Asian Blue	34
25.	Chocolate Love Delight	35
26.	Dipped in Honey	36
27.	Hazel in Nature	37
28.	Red Eyes	38
29.	And She	39
30.	Angel Behind the Glass	40
31.	Chamelula	41
32.	Can't Let It Go	42
33.	Being Broken	43
34.	Beautiful Blackness in Motion	44
35.	As Is	46
36.	Afro-Mex	48
37.	A Reflection	49
38.	I Was Finally Able	51
39.	Last Words	53
40.	Soul for a Dream	54
41.	When Darkness Hides	56
42.	Square One	57
43.	The Heart	58
44.	Our Conversations	60
45.	I Want To	61
46.	Unwrapped	63
47.	Waiting	65
48.	Turn Self-Hatred	66
49.	Wanted	68
50.	When I was Afraid to Love	69
51.	The Invisible Girl	71
52.	Let Me	72
53.	Goodnight My Love	74
54.	It's Complicated	75
55.	Father	77

Table of Contents

56. Bruised Tattoo 78
57. When God Says "No" 79
58. Déjà vu 81
59. The Color Pink 82
60. That Night 83
61. Poetic Bandit 84
62. The Beauty of a Broken Heart 85
63. First Lady Michelle 86
64. Never Have 88
65. Beautiful, Beautiful 89
66. Chocolate Dreams 90
67. Picture Of 91
68. Glass Mirror on the Wall 92
69. Forbidden 93
70. Folly 95
71. I See You In 97
72. Between the Lines 98
73. A Letter to… 100
74. Goodnight My Love 102
75. Somethings 103
76. Kingdom Man 104
77. Before Another Man 106
78. I Need to Know Before 107
79. Like 109
80. Red, Green, and Black 110
81. Brokenness 112
82. Paper Love 114
83. Defiled 116
84. Estranged 118
85. Let Someone Love You 120
86. My Virgin 121
87. Unwrapped 122
88. Toxicity 124
89. When We 125
90. Of Yesterday 126

Table of Contents

91.	Russian Roulette	128
92.	I Loved Love	130
93.	She	131
94.	Tenderness	132
95.	Ego	134
96.	Skel'leton	136
97.	Medusa	137
98.	Honeymoon, After-moon, Reality	138
99.	Mommy Don't	140
100.	Unborn plead	142
101.	Virtuous Woman	144
102.	I Went Inside	145
103.	So You Feel	146
104.	Touch	147
105.	My Secret Lover	148
106.	Nothing	150

Poisonous Ways

She was **Arsenic** in nature; she whispered her deadly toxicity-words in my hearing, penetrating my weakened soul, while lining my heart with her **Hemlock** poison-ness flowery touch while I fall into a daze of confusion, not understanding her **Dimethyl mercury** lethal touch had oppressed my immune system from fight off any invasion of destruction from her opaque presence.

I was paralyzed by her **Aconite** thoughts through her eyes and they were filled with **Polonium Radioactive** vision.

As I looked upon her vision, it caused me to lose my sight of perception as I fall to my knees in limbo, she breathes upon my presences with blows of **Mercury** setting my soul aglow with a fire.

It burned within the confines of my abode, **Belladonna** means beautiful woman.

I could not resist the lures hypnotizing features that caught me off guard long vulnerable state she feed with **Cyanide** fruit from her hands of death.

She knew that I loved seafood, so she placed before me some **Tetrodotoxin.**

My vision started to blur from the fish she hand fed me while I was in a state of hunger.

I thought she was the love of my life only to find that her intention was not love but revenge. However, her final act of what appeared to be a token of affection was her giving me **Botulinum Toxin** that paralyzed my breathing where I breathe my last breath.

Poisonous Ways.

Another Man's Hands

In my sleep, my dream, I saw another man's hands caressing the body of my beloved. As I watched for a while, it appeared I was in a trance. Nevertheless, it was more like a deep dream that was so real as though I could feel his hands touching the body of my beloved, with whom I merged with at the altar of "I do".

When two become one with another individual, you know things even when there is not even a spoken word. My spirit was trapped inside of her and wherever she went, I went too. We were connected for life.

I saw him through her eyes as he laced her lips with his. There was something about his hands as he stroked her ego with words of innuendos invitation for a night of folly and foreplay.

That night they danced with fire that burst from their blossom of their lustful displays of touch, hide and seek. His hands where the vehicle, she played the mistress with another lover with free course of her bodily possession at will.

I could see that his hands spoke the same language as I did when I was in a state of heated intoxications with the smell of her perfume. I recognized that he was a counterfeit of truth in the form of touch.

While he stroked her body with hands on instructions of foreplay as she was being led to a place of no return. He could not have untouched her and she could not lose the feeling he imprinted upon the silhouette of her heart. And while they played house for the night, I lost my sleep for a period of time trying' to figure out whether it was a hallucination of my conviction, altering my thoughts about the violations committed by my own other half. All I know is this when I saw through his hands I knew they were not mine. Another man's hand.

Little Girl

There is a little girl in there behind all that pain of broken relationships and promises. She hides behind the mask of anger to prevent anyone from executing the cycle of emotional abuse because she was emotional.

It was through feelings and sharing that she is most vulnerable since she allowed strangers of unknown origins into her world of familiarity, so they touched the very embodiment of who she was.

She was prone to trusting over and over again until she realized that only mass destruction had visited upon the very grounds, she had grown into a flower, so beautiful. Life has changed for this little girl.

Now she avoids love as if it is a plague because she was disgraced by lies of mistrust and the walls of protection have now become a fortress of denial. Not being able to face life as the once innocent heart who walked in liberty without fear.

She is wounded by the occasion of not knowing when words of truth will appear to validate who she is. The princess of life, the nurturer of nature, the healer of hope, the hand that rocks the cradle. In spite of all life's mishaps and disappointments, there is still a little girl in there who needs love and affection. Who needs to be held and often told how beautiful she really is.

She needs assurance of security and a safe place for to rest her soul during the night season of slumber.

She needs her hand held the moment she begins to take her first steps into the world of many paths.

She is precious in the eyes of all who behold her glory.

There is a little girl in there and the only time and understanding will once again cause her to come out of the shell of hibernation to show forth her presences as a beautiful butterfly.

There is a little girl in there. Little girl.

So Many Hands

So many hands have laced her body with feelings and thoughts not her own. She was unfamiliar with the tricks of the trade that paved the way into a world of forbidden experiences. She was ill prepared to handle, as her innocence has screamed for help, but no one came to her rescue.

Over the years, it became commonplace to allow touches from strangers with dark intention to buy portion of her time to express their narcissistic demeanor in private places. No longer was she a little girl with hopes and dreams, but she lived through myriads displays of nightmarish cycle of playback episodes of insane deeds.

So many hands have come and gone that she refused to feel the human side of herself.

Her job consists of her being on call 24 hours a day to sell acts of folly and lustful exploits to the highest bidder who craves her tender caress the most.

Life can never be the same since she was never claimed by a man as a daughter to protect.

She still asks the question, Where was daddy when I needed him most?

So many hands.

Black Widow

Beware of the black widow. She is out for revenge.

She is beautiful and cunning. Nevertheless, her intent is deadly. In secret, she reflects upon the many abuses she incurred over the years, after she was betrayed by love. She is driven by love, but that love has turned into lust because of the years of grueling heartache promised by the love of her life.

She is deadly and can kill at will with her asinine motives, but her death process is slow and lethal.

She been broken by lost time of giving more than she received back from pouring her heart out to a man, whose only intent was not to be faithful. Her heart became black due to the empty nights of going without the light of love. She grew into a widow after her love for the man who claimed to love her cheated over and over again, until everything she knew about love slipped right through the cracks into her shattered heart.

The memories of what use to be no longer exist. She was defiled by the touches of other lovers; she was unfamiliar with through his cold touches. She could no longer please the husband she once knew, due to his infidelity and reckless behaviors.

Black widow.

And I Reached

And I reached for her though she was full of hurt and pain: I waited silently while praying for healing. I wanted to love her unconditionally without expecting anything in return until her complete recovery from past wounds. I fell in love the moment I understood that she was the love of my life. I prayed and asked God if He could use my hands as a part of her therapeutic liberation. I was willing and able to remain by her side until the sun began to rise once again so that hope could grow without measure.

When I looked into her eyes I saw the tenderness of her spirit reaching out for me with walls of separation, but I would not be detoured. I was willing to hold on for two lifetimes if that is what it took her to say yes.

I have never known a love so deep that I was ready to commit myself to restoring her confidences for the rest of my life. Every time I walk into her presence, I can feel the essence of her being.

I know in my heart that she is the one for me and I will find a way to communion with her soul next to mine.

I know one day she will see that my love is genuine as pure gold as I continue to reach for her.

And I reached.

Almond Shape

As beautiful as they were, I saw Almond shape eye colored with honey brown deep chocolate Nubian coffee Carmel sweet suckle tint, that held my attention while I gazed upon her oval brownish vision of hope trying to figure out how I could make her reality from the desires of my imagination created for sole purpose of fulfilling the hunger of wanting to drink from the cup of wanting her so badly.

I could not help myself from staring deep into the windows of desire. Feeling the flames of passion calling my name, I had no other recourse but to pursue the history of your beginnings. I have this fetish for Almond shaped eyes, kind of drives a brother wild.

She had style that wowed my mind, went blind for a love second.

I began to back track to find her whereabouts, dispelling all the myths, catching a case of addiction.

Being hooked like a crook trying to steal some treasures, but it was more like my pleasure.

Gazing on those Almond shaped eyes, she became my prize.

Almond shape.

At the Altar

At the altar, I saw you before time arrayed in a beautiful garment of loveliness. I reached down through time and claim you as mines, and as you turned towards me at that moment, we both agreed to the possibilities of loving for a lifetime, in an eternal state of bliss. I knew you before we ever passed words of personal conversation.

After waiting all this time, I am still overwhelmed with excitement. Never a moment goes by when you do not submerge my thoughts with endless proclivities of delightful joy.

Just the mention of your name causes an explosive in my emotions; you are the source of my happiness, my sun that burns brightly all of my days and my moon that gives clarification into the very intricate fibers crafted by the Creator himself. I relish every thought of you as a gift of unconditional love bestowed upon the grounds of planting.

Every time you walk into my presences, you change the structure of my perception. Your eyes are a wonder to behold as I glare into the deepest part of your being to know you as you are beyond amazing.

Your hair is woven from that of an angel adorn with camel coffee brown that causes my heart to rejoice. Your skin is softer than silk, smoother as a newborn infant. And as I ponder upon the blessing standing before me at the altar, as I make a vow to never let a day go by when love is never absent, my arms are forever open to hold you as if I can't live without your touch.

This is my promise at the altar.

A Love I have almost had

I was searching my feelings to find my way back to love. Along this path of life, I have lost a love that has derailed my ability to interpret true love in the midst of my presence. My emotions hid themselves from any reflections of how love once danced before my eyes.

My hope was stirred to rekindle the sparking flames to burn freely without restraints naturally. I have flashbacks of moments when truth was surreal. The love I was seeking was extraordinary with a twist of mystery. Every now and then, there is resurgence of her presences. I feel the movement of her power flow like long distance telepathy permeating the air that I breathe.

The absence of her mystical touches caused a volcanic disruption in my ability concentrate upon anything long enough, but draws me continually back to her ability to keep my thoughts at bay.

As if I am imprisoned by her radioactive calls through the nighttime seasons while my visions turn into dreams paint with scented sketch of her last appearances. At times I feel the winds blowing portion of her silhouette against my soul to remind me of the once kindle flames that still burns from the residue of being loved by called beautiful.

The whole of my being gravitate through time and space to trace her whereabouts, to recapture the hope I cannot live without. Her love is liquid in form because she quenches my thirst for any other. Her love is like a solid composition because it is the only known subside to feed hungry craving pains to ease my addiction. My nights are blue without her glorious illuminous light to reveal what I saw the first time I was exposed her amazing passion. My heart beats excessively at the reoccurring memory of her ways.

It has been some time since I have held her in my arms. I would give two lifetimes for exchange for one short lifetime; *living and loving on her with all the power I possess, to reveal her my true intentions.*

A love I almost had.

Beautiful in Red

When I saw her, she was crown with a beautiful red headscarf that matched her mocha olive skin; it was as if she had been formed out of finest material unknown. I was engulfed by her appearance from the first time my eyes lay upon the reflection of her magnificence's. She captured my mind, and I became wordless for moments of time. I was intrigued and wanted to know more because my heart became restless, and I sought to understand her historical appearance. I could see a spirit of humility as she spoke softly and said hello in a gentle soothing voice. I could feel the warmth in her eyes as she gazed my way. I saw the mark of beauty, the mole that laced her face, accented her loveliness, truly, she was a princess.

She was beautiful in red, for it represented the love in her heart for all humanity. She was a dream come true in my lifetime to be privileged to look upon a glorious creation of God. It would take several lifetimes to understand her ways for she is a wonder to behold. She was like no other, for she was amazing and if the opportunity ever came to spend a space of time sharing about what was in her heart, I would be overwhelmed with compassion, I would be most grateful.

Beautiful in Red.

Before God

Before God, as we stand here at the altar of promise, I vow the ultimate pledge of sacrificial offering of giving myself to you and you along.

Before God, I said I'd do whatever it takes to ensure yours and mine happiness, until I breathe my last breath here on this earth.

Before God, I choose to walk the path of happy ever after, where I am willing to protect the love of my life until death do us part.

Before God, I swear oneness, singleness, and wholeness so that my words I've spoken before the Creator shall never be broken nor violated by any acts of dishonor that would diminish the truth I've spoken on the day I said I love you.

Before God, I hold the hand of the one I'm so in love with, staring into the eyes of my vision of hope, with this kiss I seal my soul with hers, holding her body, I will never allow another to make her feel the way I felt.

Before God, I do this that she may know; I'm the man she wanted all the days of her life, and for that, no other can touch her soul the way I do, because she is my soul mate.

Before God.

Before We Sleep

Before we sleep there is a few things I want to say.

Before we fall into a daydreaming night of repeated pictures of what transpired during time as we walked among the living conversing about things that mattered, things of the heart that would keep us apart but coming together is a sign of trying to weather everything that brings disaster holding the relationship together because we made a choice to stay with each other my lover.

Before we sleep, I want to make sure there's no open door to allow separation of our hearts.

Before we sleep, I want to talk about the things that concern thee my sweet hear the words of my heart, words of my dreams, words of truth my desire is to be with you.

Before we sleep.

Betrayal

*L*ove said to be of a betrayal nature is not love, but hate disguised to trick the ears and eyes, but for a moment of time until truth rises from the bed of transparency to discern between passion or someone faking words of the imagination.

Love hidden from the heart will only send out signals of warning that something is terribly wrong, but one must first be in touch with their own feeling, not spending too much time neglecting the signs or the handwriting on the walls of their hearts, eating away at the very conscious that guards them from hurt, harm and danger, lurking is a prankster, tricksters trying implore one's mind to turn the tide in their favor.

Love is not born with heinous and deplorable nature.

Love believes all things, love trust its intuition, love is not blind, it sees very clearly.

Love has no boundaries when opening its arms and live to protect that which is dear to its own heart.

Many would say they love you in words only, but love is an action verb, it walks the walk and talk the talk.

Beware of those that say they love with an empty heart.

Betrayal.

Black Rose

My **black rose**, the darkness of your pedals led to me the down the path of passionate love, causing me to fall into the **black** hole of your heart.

I long for you like water in the dessert thirsty and parched, needing your liquid love to survive in the heat of this life. Your mysterious ways drew me to the root of your beginning. As your stem grows deep in the fertile soil of my compose I feel the growth of your stems reaching deep into my fertile earth.

I feel you extending your territory through the space of my continuation longing to understand the movement of your soul.

My **black rose** I love how you make me feel when I look upon the deep dark **velvet** soft texture of your leaves. Like silk, my hands glide over you with caring caresses of adoration. My **black rose** you are one of a kind, as if no other can make me wonder why you are so unique and beautiful.

I love you my **black rose** always and forever.

Black Rose.

BLACK SPICE

As I remembered on Christmas Eve in December, she was like **black** spice draped in somebody fittin' tights, just right for the occasion, her ruby red lips were just right for kissin', causin' an explosion in the emotions.

I was holdin' on for dear life, she was about five-foot somethin' take or add a few inches mo', and when she spoke, I knew she was bi-lingual with a smooth conversation that was intriguing, as I started reasoning in my mind, I knew it was gonna take a little time because the girl was refined like fine wine.

Her hair was like **black** silk woven from the hand of an Angel, she was born with a mocha deep dark chocolate skin that pulled on my inter craving to touch the beauty of creation, her lips were perfectly laced with crimson love, her eyes were colored with mahogany cinnamon brown hazelnut tint, reflecting the mystery of her vision, she was an amazing form of loveliness exposed to the eye of the beholder, she was like **black** spice tea with essence of Nubian favor taste, she was kind of like a mixture of fantasy and reality all in one, I was hypnotized when I looked upon her silhouette, like the goddess Medusa who turned the hearts of men to stone but **black** spice turns the hearts of men to learn about the history of her beginnings, she was like black spice.

Black spice.

Come Here

Come here and let me hold you in my arms so I can feel the texture of your surface. I need to know something deeper than the mere appearance of you standing over there. The distance between us does not allow me to taste the scent of your presence.

I can read your movement as you draw closer to me, and something is causing an allergic reaction in my heart. I cannot help but watch your eyes as they rotate back and forth like a beautiful melody being sung while you approach the zone of approval.

There is a chemical explosion formulating inside the shell of our existence, which contains all that we are. I feel a weakening of my will as my hand touched your skin. For a moment of time, I lost my sense of reality as I was transported into yours. I saw and felt every emotion you have ever known in the soulish experience.

I felt like I was on a rollercoaster ride to heaven, riding through the waves of your love you dispelled. Your love is the color of gold, pure and crystal clear.

I never known passion so deep that when I began to drown in the mist of your possibilism; it lifted me up higher and higher, never wanting to come down from your mountaintop. Now that I have experience, the highs and the deep lows of your world, I feel like we can never be separated ever again. Moreover, as I descend back to reality. I have known what it is to have been truly loved.

Come here.

Yellow Dress

I remember the bright yellow dress she wore that summer eve. It was like the color of fluorescent love shining so bright that night. A special moment in time past, I shall never forget.

The winds blew softly as it whispered its tender cries of calm between us, while the breeze of freedom set upon us to run free. That night we sat upon an old couch on the back porch while having an intimate conversation about how I wanted her body, soul and spirit. Her words were like animated life, frozen in a space of time, anchoring my thoughts for the moment when liberated love would be expressed without restriction or any regrets.

When she smiled, the stars began to explode like firecrackers on the fourth of July, to celebrate her beautiful existence. While gazing into her vision, it became apparent to me that I had found the fountain of eternal life. She made me feel like I was born again for a second time, forever.

It was almost unbelievable to know that one had the power to give such a gift to one seeking the truth about love. Her touch was as if God himself had come down from heaven in human form to reveal real unconditional, sacrificial, and selfless un-incarcerated revelation to help me comprehend the price of love.

The yellow dress has stained my memory forever. I am continuously imprisoned with joy and pain, wisdom and understanding. The loss of her presences has caused pain, but the remembrance of the yellow dress has restored my joy.

Yellow dress.

Shades of Orange

Her skin was painted with a **Burnt Orange** hue draped in loveliness kissed by the Sun while creation was deciding the depth of her perfection, before the profound appearance of being exposed to the light as it reveals her true inter beauty.

While her **Rust** colored eyes glisten like the fall times when leaves changes colors, so does her eyes when joy enters her heart, and she smiled because she was overwhelmed with happiness.

Her hair resembled **Champagne**, light in color but soft in texture, adored by the angels of heaven wishing they too were cherished with such fine silk hair that would make anyone envious.

Her mood was like **Tangerines** settling down like the Sun descending beneath the ocean as the world turns on its axis only to repeat the cycle repeatedly.

As the winds of life began to blow, her scent flowed through the air like the fragrance of fresh **Pumpkin** filling the air with love and life. She was gentle as a freshly picked **Peach** from the garden of eternal hope, using her healing hand to set a nation free. She is the essences of an **Apricot**, sharing the exquisiteness of her outer self with those who never knew the power liberty. She represented the many shades of Orange.

Shades of Orange.

Pale Flower

She was like an apparition with no past, transparent as an invisible mirage floating through life, I was mesmerized by the materialization of her tender complexion, it was a transformation of my emancipation of believing in the supernatural, she reminded me of the replica in my dreams, as I tried to imprison her captive presences with my hypnotic words of compassion, my words levitated through the atmosphere, chasing the scent of her whereabouts, this beautiful pale flower spoke in several languages of love, the movement of her eyes were like crystal clear Axinite Stones carved and set in place on the first day she opened her vision to the world, my heart was crystallized when I sensed her thoughts drifting through time lost moment, and I was able to decipher her multifarious linguistic communication through radio airwaves via telecommunication, her invisible soul was filled with a glass like substances that glowed with a **green** like ingredients with every movement of her systematized body that transported through unknown dimension of time and space travel.

Pale flower.

Love in Purple

I love your wine-colored eyes draws me into the secret chambers of your heart, keeping me intoxicated with your presences. I feel your mood permeating the air, like the relaxing scent of lilac, leading me down the path of your truth. I will follow you until the end of our beautiful journey into Heaven's gates.

Your love is like the setting of sun, dipped in lavender liquid with a sweet perfume aroma that fills the air of our breath, like tasting purple passion. Your kiss tastes like the ripest tender sweet plum picked from the tree of your beginning.

I love when your eyes turn a shade of mauve on a beautiful night in the summer. I am amazed at how you have captured my love down through the years. There is no one on GOD's green earth I rather spend the rest of my days loving and holding you as we walk by sea of our love. No other has touched my life in such a profound way before I met you.

You are the essence of my existences, the hope of my vision. Your love is like purple, the color of royalty.

When I look into your eyes, I realize you are the prize for which I sought after all my life. I have never known a love as beautiful as your amethyst heart. Our love will stand the test of time.

All my life I dreamed of such a day, when you and I would walk the isle of commitment to take the eternal vow of in-separation. We were destined to be together before time began and now, we must cross over threshold of no return, for we can no longer return to our formal state because our love has transformed us from the inside out. My love for you will only grow stronger and stronger as time settle in our souls and the stars call us by name.

My beloved, for always and forever.

Love in **purple**.

LOVE AND WAR

It was during wartime that they met two lovers who fell in love with passion beyond the imagination. Willing to defy the norm, they touch one another with passionate fire, creating a flame with no one to blame for being hungry for love, they glided into each other's arms and made love that created a little her.

She was as beautiful as the morning star glowing with the flow of love in her eyes. She was kept secret because she was a lovechild. Her mother was as lovely as the wild winds that blows the secrets of intimacy on a cozy cool summer eves. Her father was birth from the red clay of the earth, strong and untamed. Who could blame him for giving deep love to a young woman in search of unconditional love?

He was a "code talker" one who had the ability to decipher codes and languages. He also could discern when love was drawing him into the secret chambers of unrestrained tender affection. The attraction of them both was irresistible, almost like being out of control, never ever able to overcome the temptations to touch bodies for a moment of pleasure. It was love shared during a time of war and uncertainty.

The memories of this gentle kind man have left a legacy upon the heart of that little girl as she remembered the fond thoughts of daddy. As time winged and began to move like a vapor of mist, he passed on to the four winds, but not forgotten.

He has left an indelible mark upon the hearts of those that loved him most, that beautiful little girl. Though their relationship was forbidden, the flame never ceased to burn even in the midnight of their separate paths. Though she searched for him years later but time had expired his place here on this earth. Nothing in this life can replace the longing and the love for another individual. She still holds the memory in her heart for a piece of the past to keep hope alive. It was during wartime that love found its way into the heart of two lovers who truly never benefited from being together experiencing love to its fullest extent being together for a lifetime but they say, "All is fair in love and war."

Love and War.

B<small>LUE</small> C<small>RYSTAL</small>

*A*s I began to dig through life archives, I found this amazing blue crystal beneath the surface crest of life, isolated in a hidden place. I was overwhelmed with elation to discover this amazing wonder. No one saw what I saw within this silhouette of magnificence beautiful blue crystal stone.

The shape of her formation intrigued me. I took both hands and dusked off the debris encased around her freedom. I stroked her outer layers with gentle caresses of obsessions, protection, to ensure her safety. She was filled with a burst of mood changing color that entrapped my attention like an addiction to a psychotropic drug.

I could not help myself from staring, glaring into her atmospheric cloud of joy and happiness. She was the greatest discovery I've ever known to be exposed to my human eyes. It was more than a curious mind that caused me to put her into an undisclosed location, until I could come back at night to do a deeper, but more thorough investigation into this secret discovery.

I want to do a surveillance check to find out how and why she was alone an unprotected. When I touch the outer surface of her space, there was movement from within. As I thought, I saw the beginning of life for the first time. I kept the blue crystal hidden from public view because every time I whispered words of passion, she would glow like fluorescence liquid flowing from her glass crystal container. She was encased with a layer of truth that changed my whole perspective about her value. My discovery has been the greatest of all time, finding this once in a lifetime encounter of mines.

Blue Crystal.

Beyond My Color

Beyond the color boundaries of my skin is a world undiscovered unknowns. A world where revelations have not been revealed. A place where truth is hidden from all biases, stereotypes, and ignorance's. A place of untraveled treasures, goldmine of riches untold.

Many will never be exposed to the highly guarded archives of wisdom and knowledge. Beyond the color of my skin awaits a discovery of one of God's greatest creations ever created in this lifetime. For GOD has handcrafted a masterpiece, very few will ever come to know exist except if He reveals it Himself. Beyond the color of my skin are hopes and dreams that will change the lives of many, if given the opportunity to be embraced.

Beyond the color of my skin are shades of beautiful lights and dark hues, reflecting the diversity of my abilities. My creativity is second to none, when mixed with faith and hope. Many cannot look beyond the walls of colorless hopeful triumph measures, to reach for the glory of GOD's blessing. Beyond the color of my skin, they would only wonder, pondering how the manifestation of GOD's infinite power to making someone so great, and yet hated, because of their perception of insignificant underscores GOD's magnificence, is beyond their ability understanding comprehend manifestation at its best.

Beyond my color.

ASIAN BLUE

There are no words to describe her Asian Blue soul. She was from a world mixed with purple and red, this blended into Asian Blue. As I looked upon her formation, there were a variety of colors intermingled together to reveal her velvet smooth surface. When the sun gazed upon the exterior of her casing of bronze hues, I saw the glory of her devotion. There was an insatiable desire to know, to understand her purpose for being, she was an unexplainable enigmatic. Her surreptitious smile bore the resemblance of an exploding star, raining white phosphorus all over my visualization, giving me more clarity about her intricacies of her schematic's nature.

She was named Asian Blue because she lived in a place where life was simple and Cherry Blooms flowers grow freely to express the depths of her deep crimson love. Her beautiful streams of **black** lacquer locks draped over the shoulders of her physique blew my mind, as I was observing her architectural edifice, she moved with sophistication. Her hands turned milk chocolate color when I touched the palms. I then felt the addiction of her sugared favor scent permeating the room as she passed by my way, my eyes turned into the colors of the rainbow, rotating on the axis of my discernment. Asian Blue is a modern-day phenomenon. Truly, I have beheld the glory of her manifestation only to live and forever tell others about what I saw on that beautiful day when she appeared before me.

Asian Blue.

Chocolate Love Delight

Chocolate Love Delight so sweet you gotta have it every night to fight the addiction that sends crazy chocolate lovers on missions trying to retain the attention of their beloved Chocolate Delight love is the kind of love that lovers crave during a love crisis to help with the chocolate delight disorder you got to be borderline choc-schiz-o-matic fanatic the kind of chocolate fever that there's no relieve for trying to break down some doors just to score some healing for this type of feeling to stop the pain that killing ya so if you don't get hook you won't be diagnosis as crook trying to survive to this chocolate love crazes, hey!

If you cannot handle the chocolate, leave it alone and move on to something new. Do not be no fool when they tell you just take a little bit, and everything will be all right.

Learning from others' mistake you won't have those midnight shakes so shake yo' self off this Chocolate love delight fever.

Chocolate love delight.

Dipped in Honey

Her fingers were dipped in honey, sprinkled with confectioner sugar, underneath a layer of melted chocolate flowing from the heat wave from her body temperature.

Her fingers moved with rhythm and rhymes, as they danced across my lips. As I began to lick from her instruments of mass pleasures. One on one, as I took my time to swallow the whole finger, while enjoying the sweetness lanced upon every finger that wiggled for attention, from the stroking of my tongue. I was overwhelmed by the free addiction, beckoning unto to me to partake with liberty; the coding of love was painted upon the extended extensions of the palms of her hands.

The honey that dripped from her fingers was like an elixir syrup flowing downward slowly along the stems of my demands. There is nothing more exciting than a set of fingers, decorated with passionate mad love.

I was drawn by the sweet suckle mellow sugary smell that paralyzed my senses, as I gazed upon her sticky tentacles sculptured with myriads of rotating colors with favors dipped in honey sweet as liquid gold that melts in the mouth not in the hand.

Dipped in honey.

Hazel in Nature

The origination of her eyes was hazel in nature. A light brownish color that is reflected when the sun spreads its warmth upon the mirrors of her vision. Her eyes reveal a truth when her eyelids rise from the position closure from a night of rest from chasing her dreams. Her eyes are the portal into a world of unseen displays of passionate ambition residing in her soul.

The color hazel is manifestations of mixing diversity to create a hybrid of faded yellows and coffee browns to expose the creation of hazel tint that gives off a beautiful picture of love. The moment I saw her amazing eyes the encrypted code caught my attention.

I was enumerated by the appearance of such magnificence. There were no words to express what I saw except I was privilege to experience that moment of pleasure in the time I was allowed to behold such a wonder. To my amazement, I saw something that caused me to ponder about the reflection of her manifestation.

Hazel in nature.

Red Eyes

When I gazed into your deep **crimson** vision, I saw your vulnerability. I was willing to touch your nakedness with mines to understand what real intimacy is really like. I could feel the deep moans of your craving and it intrigues my thirst to drink from your well of pleasures. I could feel the heat rising from the vessel of your dwelling. I was excited and anxious to learn about what I saw through an accidental exposure of your innermost desire. Through your **infrared** eyes, I could see a hunger for than a momentary thrill, but you wanted to be filled with real love and affection. I wanted to be the one with the privilege of taking my time to address every need untapped by another. I knew it would be someone with skilled hands to surgically touch all the places that needed sensitive attention.

But first, you are going to have to be sedated with words of a professional, one who could sooth the wild salvage hunger that roams within your soul. I was ready to give you an aphrodisiac inoculation shot of tender caressing before putting you totally under. I knew that you had to be comma induced so there would be no pain but only pleasure. In addition, when you awaken, your spirit would be healed, so that love could once again flow freely.

Red Eyes.

And She

And she was all that and a bag of chips. Moreover, I want to kiss her innocence of purity, the freedom of being sexy and she is wonderful, marvelous and supernatural with beautiful eyes.

It is no surprise everybody wants to know what kind of inner lacking flow she throws around with natural ways. She is grounded she being found to be something special, the treasure of a king ransom worth her weight in gold, that is pure gold, so I stare because I'm aware that if I speak I should forever hold my peace but I'm moved, I perceive she got groove I knew I wanted.

I needed to be cool, and she is my supreme my dream of a lifetime awaking my Spirit to fly to the highest heavens the more I see of her the more I want.

And she.

Angel Behind the Glass

*A*ngel behind the glass of separation of two worlds.

The world of giving and receiving and as we make a covenant and agreement, we can both share, there is a transformation of hope for the both of us, knowing that we shall meet in the distant future to continue to touch the object of need, to see, to speak, to hear the words of comfort Angel behind the glass is always up to date with the latest information on every occasion.

Like a reformation of new technology setting, the people free to do, to go on to the next level of

Business furthering their future to make progress and every time we meet there is a need to verify

Who.

I am to ensure that I receive the help necessary to continue the relationship possible for growth, and as we touch for the last time and depart, we know in our heart it is not the last time we shall say bye.

Angel behind the glass.

Chamelula

Chamelula is her name because her identity is hidden between colors and the belief that she has the liberty to be whatever her heart's desire, but it is her desire to be free of all restrains that would hold her hostage to any one's belief but her own.

She has the ability to transform herself and she is filled with more than one language to interpret the cultures and the languages of others.

She is beautiful and filled with diverse worlds of understanding, loves and pains, all at the same time. She is a wonder to behold. Her mind is filled with the curiously to learn about marvelous and untapped knowledge that can only be possessed by one who is willing to venture beyond the boundaries of her fear, the walls of her imprisonment and the traditions birth in her soul before she was born.

Chamelula has a heart of gold, the treasure of a queen. She is significant to every life that shares her ways of interpretation of life. Her ways are unpredictable, but her eyes never lie, and they always tell the truth.

She is one of a kind to change hearts and minds. Chamelula moods reflect the many colors and personalities she needs to touch every need of humanity from dark to light. Born with a gift just to be herself is more than enough for the entire world to see and believe as she continues to be.

Chamelula.

Can't Let It Go

I thought long ago I had let it go, but my memory reminded me of the secret flames still burning with fervent passion for one I lost so long ago. I thought another could replace her with time, I thought. But, in reality, nothing has really changed but the passing of time.

I still see the most amazing smile that a woman could ever wear on one so lovely. Her eyes were the path into my future, but somehow life stole my dreams through mishap and deception. I never thought I could really live without her, but with the absence of her touch, I lost my vison in time.

I had to endure a life of living without the one thing that cause me to rise every morning with hope of seeing, feeling, and loving on my queen.

I am a king who has been without a queen for so long that my heart has imprisoned itself from any attempts to allow the love me it holds so deeply to be experienced by another. Only the one who has the key to unlock this treasure whom it is meant for can hold the heat that would consume others, and the passionate flicker for her still burns out of control. Some things in life are meant to be let go, but true love is not one of them. My soil is the planting of her gene in my soul, how could I have ever let her go. I have learned to embrace the visuals of her silhouette, keeping my hope alive.

Can't let it go.

Being Broken

Being broken ain't easy, like a piece of glass, which fell to the ground and shattered into many pieces, a separation of self, of feeling, of memories.

Even a separation of healing, trying to reconnect is a job at best, where there use to be synergy, now there's less energy, being broken is a token of life's disappointments, having your heart broken by a mother, a father's, a brother or another, no protection of love in this cold world.

On the other hand, what I heard curbed my belief that there is some relieve to set me free. To put me back together again, through the help of friends.

Find a friend, you find healing, find healing, you will find mending, find mending, you'll find deliverance, find deliverance, you'll find your true place again, going from broken to wholeness once again.

Being Broken.

Beautiful Blackness in Motion

Her blackness was full of life and amazement, as she began to create from her own fashion, only one could have imagined that she would birth it from the vision of her beginnings, as she was destined to reign as queen amongst queens, she would bring forth life through her hand as part of the Master plan.

To give insight into her gift that was in great demand, her love for sewing would be hand crafted according to the curves of the girls and the ladies that would drive a brother crazy.

From her mind, she drew colors and prints that would be evident that her beautiful blackness was in motion, as the women walk the down the aisle one at a time, to move with spirit and the groove of the Nile River flowing in and out to and fro, making a brother want some more of her designs because she was beautiful and so fine, as she began to create once again, the revelation flowed in measure untold because her colors were beautiful and bold, her ability to call upon the artistic gift that would create rift into the industry as something supernatural as being heaven made, so they say, with different sizes, colors and shapes of the female gender world cause a stir in the minds of those who stared with excitement, as the prized gowns were life to the lovely sister that strolled down the walkway, everybody was filled with thrills, because the garments are beautifully priced, so tonight will be a moment to remember as the gorgeous women of beautiful blackness are in motion.

Beautiful Blackness in Motion

As Is

As we venture into new relationships it is a time of excitement and intrigue, wondering about all the wonderful discoveries we will find on our journey to apprehend the unknowns of relationships.

In our minds we have this believe of "perfection" which looks right, feels right, sounds right, it is our perceptions and realities of our own experiences that bring us to a place of final verdicts, of this is it, when in an imperfect world, we have concluded that, that which we're pursuing will suffice all of our desires for love, hope, and security.

Entering into a new relationship is like buying a new used vehicle, it is perfect for you until you had it for a while and you began to see things you never saw, things you never noticed before entering into an agreement to purchase it.

Your feeling begins to somewhat change, because of little things you really were not expecting to find.

When one enters into a relationship, you have agreed to the "as is clause" and all the imperfections that come along with being committed to that "one stop shop relationship. There will be times when one will desire to return the relationship back to the place from which they found it. However, they did not read the fine print, which says, "Final purchase no refund, clearance sale no returns."

Caught up in the moment of ecstasy, all they know is "I want it," no matter the cost. One cannot change the intended purpose for which something is created, or you cannot go into a relationship thinking that you are going to change the way an individual is. You are headed down the road of "disaster." There will be things one likes about the relationship and there will be things one does not like about the relationship, point blank.

Before one enters into a long-term agreement or relationship, one must do the homework if they expect to get the most for their time and effort of love. To be happy is to be willing to accept one as is and be adoptable to change different from what one has known in the past.

Leave the past behind and work on the present. If you bring past failure and mindsets into the present relationship, you will receive the same old' results, nada, or nothing. Begin the relationship on the premises that it is an exciting and that you want to get the most out of it. If you look for the good things, you will find all the beauty the mind can behold. If you go in the relationship with honest expectation, you will not be disappointed. If you go in ready to give with a pure heart, you shall receive your heart desire. Remember this one thing and you will do well. Love the individual like you want to be love and they will give the same.

As is.

Afro-Mex

Afro-mex, a combination of two fluently living side by side, dark but light, two but one, separately they have two distinct personalities yet the same struggles, to make it in a society that denies notoriety, trying to rise above the poverty level and the mainstream turns around and gives them a shovel, a sign of hard labor headed for an early grave, but truth will save the day, revelation will exalt them, wisdom has taught them.

If two become one it's the total sum of synergy, where the individual part were divided less strength to commence with the evidences, now coming together to shatter all stereo-types, to grind the mind of Big Brother causing him to rethink his strategy , to keep the people incarcerated, now like the rising of the sun, the birthing of a nova, the finding of a new planet the people rise in Unisom to say we are one, though we have differences yet we agree to be free to partake in the all the privileges like the rest , the best haven't been told until we unfold as

Afro-Mex.

A Reflection

I miss the tender touch of your whispering gentle words, speaking softly to a hungry soul needing the flow of your lovely sounds of hope.

Like no other, the twinkle in your eyes give off a sweet honey scent that is evident that your heart is about to explode with emotional gestures of needing so much more than the natural, but the supernatural, one moment of staring into your eyes would cause a gazing over of my peripheral vision, seeking to know the essences of your existence, the waves of your vibes set my mind ablaze with flaming flames of emerald bluish red reflection of your amazing presences, my thirst to sip from your cup of mystery causes my heart to dance to the sound of your breath as you exhale with desire.

I feel the heat of your vulnerability open up to love without restrictions, only needing your permission to execute the mission that is before me, waiting patiently until you beacon. Until love can longer abide alone, searching for a home to express its fullest power of unconditional giving, walking in freedom to be all you want to be, you alone have the power to create your world of joy, time ticks with certainty, while we wrestle in our memories, the hunger grows stronger and stronger, our thought are simply reflections of our inter craving, as we ponder upon what might be and what is, life is wonderful and whom we care for means the world to us, the sun smiles all day long in anticipation of your appearance, the moon beams with the thoughts of your tender like velvet silk leather skin freshly washed in baby oil mixed with lavender, your hair I long to brush with that of an Angels brush, gliding my hands along your silk's strands of your beauty, I give thanks for who you are.

A reflection

I Was Finally Able

I was able to let her go after imprisoning her in my thoughts for a life sentence.

I held on to her for so long that no other could have ever occupy my heart long enough to experience the deep passionate touches.

I have longed to give to the one deserving of real love, but my heart became frozen in time with no way to escape the self-incarceration I built around my feelings.

She had saturated, penetrated the whole of my being with the influence of her touch, kisses, and smile. I was intoxicated with the thought of her being mines for a lifetime.

In my dreams, I saw her lying in my arms as we traded feeling and emotions.

She became mines because we agreed in those moments to express the highest form of intimacy.

In my dreams I saw that she had moved on after being after being absent from love lost so long ago.

I saw that she was happy and I was able to let go of her completely.

It was the longest love affair I've ever had without love of my life present.

I now have peace knowing that she found love once again.

I was finally able.

Last Words

I remember our last conversation we had so many years ago. I was rehearing in my memory your thought you shared before we would depart for a lifetime.

My heart has been trapped by the emotions we shared in time past.

You asked if I loved you and my answer was yes that I would always love you.

My greatest struggles have been living without you and not being able to hold you in my arms.

The sound of your soft southern voice resonated in the soul of my existences. I wish that the last words I spoke to you had been the consolation you needed to maintain our connection for a lifetime.

I wish I could turn back the hands of time to rekindle the fire that ran through out veins like liquid Nitroglycerin. Your words have defined my perception of love.

Your touch as I remember was so comforting to one experiencing real love for the first time. Your last words were painted on my subconscious for a love time of living in a world where so few have not discovered the art loving on an exponential level.

Last words.

Soul for a Dream

I was offered a dream for the price of a soul and the ultimate goal was to exchange one for the other. I have longed to see my world on the inside, manifested on the outside into my reality where dreams are only dreams if they stay locked up within the confines of my mind.

But there was an invitation through revelation written in word form, that in a small amount of time that which I so long waited to see if it could be expedited quickly by the power and influence of another who had the means and know how to escort my vison right before my eyes.

I was almost tempted to ask why one would want to aid another in giving life to a dream that was not their own, though I was aware that there would be a cost incurred upon swearing my allegiances to a cause with its own merits.

Nothing is ever free; many have sold their souls for temporary moments while the pleasures of fame would only last until the expiration. This short-lived life and then why would I be able to at the end of my turn in life would my dream back in exchange while drifting into the next life.

Would I have time to reverse my decision while life was trying to flee into a different dimension from the natural to spiritual? After seeking, what I perceived the deal of a lifetime would not bring me the joy I assumed was happiness. To sell oneself for a fantasy will eventually turn out to be the worst decision ever.

Could I break my contract with the Devil after signing my name in blood? Blood covenants are some the most difficult after you been convinced that what you're doing is right, but greed and power always corrupts individuals that doesn't understanding the power of relationships.

Soul for a dream.

When Darkness Hides

I have seen darkness concealed in the disguise of deceptive light of invitation amusing the heart of unsuspecting watchers of the truth.

Light always exposes that which is opposite of itself revealing the true identity of covert lies living amongst revelation.

When darkness hides, it tries to cover up its diabolical evil intent to destroy the masses in order to control the dictates of humanity. It's only reason for existing is to transform the light into darkness.

Darkness is the nemesis of all that is good. When darkness hides, its only purpose is to look innocent as if someone is trying to pickpocket someone while their hand is sliding out of the packet and they get caught "Red handed".

We must learn that walking in truth and that truth is light. There is power in transparency, but there is great danger when darkness hides.

When Darkness Hides

Square One

It seems like we always end up back at square one. Life is like a maze trying to find our way to a place beyond a place where life makes sense.

Trying to press beyond mediocre mere existences does not measure up to our expectation of being free to live a life without all the struggles.

It is almost as if we are trapped in a cycle of limitation where we have reached the highest level of living in the heavenly zone.

It is kind of walking in a place where the mountains are unclimbable, impassable, out of reach of our potential grasp for something greater than our present circumstances.

Square one deems to be a familiar place for those who cannot seem to break the chain of bondage where one becomes accustomed to the laws and rules that dictate the present moment of life.

An invisible maze is made up of transparent walls that feels impenetrable to human effort, like traveling in the wilderness only to walk pass the familiar landmarks that never seems to change.

Square one.

The Heart

No matter how you try to give the heart something that seems like love it can tell the difference.

The heart can discern when true love is present or something that appears to be a counterfeit is there.

Love knows the butterflies when they fly in the inter recesses of the soul.

Love given a voice will declare with its own words that it has found something it feels and know is real.

The heart goes through different expression of what may look like love. It often experiences something called "lust"; you cannot always trust lust for it is self-contain and puta a drain on the heart. If it takes and never gives, but fends for its own survival, give, give me, all about me. Selfishness takes the very life out of the soul.

Something else called "infatuation", in my estimation; it is kind of like love until it comes to the reality that love takes work and can be exhausting when having to give when it doesn't feel like.

Another I've notice is something called a "Crush", it hangs around for a while until it comes down from its high like a roller-coaster only to show itself as unstable until the cable of communication brake and runs wild.

It will for a while only to disappear into thin air leaving you wondering if it really cared to be just there for a free ride until it dies.

The thing about it is real and one can feel the power of its presences.

It will never hide, nor is it disguised, as being something it is not.

It is like a flower that blooms into something beautiful with time.

Real love is patient and kind, it loves to take time when expressing it's true nature.

It does not fake it, but keeps it real, the heart knows the differences and it won't accept anything less than the real "McCoy".

The Heart.

Our Conversations

Our conversations have been filled with transparency of lives broken by life and time only to be healed by revelation and one's personal experience.

Our conversations have been filled with unconditional acceptances of one another's past interactions with the darkness that besiege us all at one time or another.

Our conversations have at moments has caused our emotions to feel beloved affection that all humanity so desire to be expressed between souls that longed for a touch in a world lacking intimacy.

Our conversations have lead us to a place of revealing history only private to the one giving the other permission to share in their personal knowledge precious to themselves.

Our conversations have been words spoken about how pain and disappointments that has evaporated over time only to leave a better understanding of how beautiful life really is after the storms of life have come and gone.

Our conversations have been filled with purple moon and green sun shines illuminating the many feeling in our hearts creating a world of meaningful conversation.

Our conversations

I Want To

I want to taste your soul through my lips as I kiss the essences of your existences.

I want to feel the intense heat of your ways.

I want to hold the strong fires of your desires.

I want to feel the palms of your hands as I glide upon the texture of my manliness that I might know your deep thoughts.

I want to dance with your silhouette until the sun begin to rise from its resting place.

I want to feed from the hunger that rages within the walls of our incarceration.

I want to sip from your wells that I might never thirst again.

I want to read your thought from the inside out, reading your memoirs of love.

I want to caress your emotions while flowing from your heart to mines.

I want to hear the whispers of your melodic tones as you speak from depths of comforting words.

I want to hold you with bars of stealth conversations to let you know that you live in the arms of safety.

I want to.

Unwrapped

Like a present being unwrapped, I took my time to dishcloth her unwanted disappointments to replace them with approval. I was careful not to pull or tug too hard because I did not want to tear anything vital to her healing.

I want to be the balm that heals from the outside in and from the inside out once, I have moved pass the barriers of restriction that would forbid me from entering into the private sector of her life.

I know I need a high security clearance to behold such sensitive information only privy to the possessor of precious treasure.

Before, I touch her, I will consecrate my hands with love so that there will not be any contamination of unwanted intimacy illuminating around as she began to expose her glory to me.

I want to handle her with express care, overnight propriety and ensure her safety with being unwrapped without any damage to the content of her vulnerability.

She needs to know that the hands that hold her tender substances will not crush or squeeze, but she will be pleased with the caressing of her goods. She then needs to know the one who is qualified to uncover her most secret place where she is open to receiving unconditional love with affection.

I know that she is fragile and I must go slowly when touching the surface of her beginning to stop any apprehension of care. As I guild my hands upon her tender soul, she will then know that it is okay.

And she will lay there without fear until I am done with removing all the covering that covers up her beauty.

Unwrapped.

Waiting

While waiting, I am anticipating something new. I can only imagine how wonderful it's gonna be.

I feel this joy in my heart; it is a feeling kind of like meeting love for the first time. I am so excited that my feelings are about to explode into ecstasy.

Like being on a roller coaster ride, ridin' real high. I'm gonna take my time, almost like drinking a glass of wine.

And when the time comes, I am gonna greet her with words of passion she cannot even imagine and what I'm gonna do to win her heart.

I am just waiting for the moment in time when I blow her mind. I am gonna do something to change her philosophy of intimacy.

I call her freedom because she will allow me to take her in my arms and put on the charm.

I cannot wait until we dance for the first time, and I look into her eyes. While I'm holding her close it will be a time of toasting her existence, for me it's gonna be a time of reminiscing about how this love affair gonna play out.

But for the night, I will just wait until she says yes to pass the test of seeking for true love. So, I will just wait.

Waiting.

Turn Self-Hatred

Turn the philosophy of self-hatred into self-love.

If one cannot love themselves, they cannot love others.

Years of counseling people who have no self-worth accepted the free labor they were co-cohered to give by force and intimidation.

Those who promote hatred are those who hate themselves the most.

How can people proclaim that GOD is a righteous GOD and just GOD, and yet they commit evils against humanity that would cause. GOD to be ashamed and say, "How can this be".

I understand why so many people question authenticity of GOD's power and love. It is because of what they were made to believe and that it was the will of GOD to utterly implement stages of genocide against people GOD deems lower than animals.

It is amazing how certain people can speak for GOD when HIMSELF cannot attest to they are testimony.

Self-hatred is birthed out of the hearts of men who placed themselves in the place of GOD and judge only today find themselves before the true and living GOD giving an account of the crimes they said they thought HE would approve only to be rejected and given a life sentence for committing perjury against the Most-high.

Self-hatred reflects a teaching handed down for centuries to keep a people in bondage for profit. Let the shackles be broken and hatred on transform into love.

Turn self-hatred.

Wanted

She wanted to be free, but she did not possess the right of freedom. Incapacitated by the dastardly deeds of the master his only desires were to force his darkest folly upon her at will but could not kill her will to be free.

She could see that her body was nothing more than a toy for his ploy of mind games that bought confusion and distillation to her world. Daily, she inadvertently was deprived of spoken to with words of hate and yet she dreamed of being loved and not used and abused by someone lustful hatred of another human being to only satisfy the demons lust of another and his humanity is questionable.

Born into a world where she was bought for a few dollars to the highest bidder at an auction with her goods being on public display so that others could look upon the investment that could bring years of free labor and sex to do as the master pleased.

But deep within her heart, she knew the difference between lust and love. They took from her, her self-respect and stole her identity by force, but they were never able to kill her truth about real love.

Wanted.

When I was Afraid to Love

*I*t is only when I reflect upon the pain of yesterday's. Every attempt to love unconditionally without the retribution of affliction.

When I was exposed to the abuse as a young child it set, the tone atmosphere how I would perceive real love.

But, it was not love, it was resentment, bitterness and emotional impure to touches from impure hands.

I did not understand what genuine love was until I saw the sacrifice of Christ. The one who would pay the price for my life. "Greater love has no man or savior than he then He who would lay down His life for a friend or loved one".

I needed the lover of my soul to set me free from my misery. My heart was shackled with things and filled with shame that blinded with from liberty to live a life of tranquility.

Perfect love cast out all fear, for fear has torment. I went from darkness to light in my lifetime, to know and understand what love would look and feel like.

Love is more than a feeling, but an action. It does not talk a good game; it shows in deeds and action.

No longer am I afraid to love because it has the power to heal; the power to set men free and change destinies. The characteristic of love is never irritated; puffed up; it is never rude; it will never holds grudges. But always forgiving and it never remembers other people's faults.

Fear is a constant reminder that I should be cautious about my heart being out of sync with truth. It has been said, "You shall know the truth and the truth shall set you free if you wanna be".

As we become free; we must set others free.

When I was afraid to love.

The Invisible Girl

I often see her when she is not visible to the plain eyes, but I can see her thru my transparency vision that is undetectable by others. I feel her movement every time her soul wonders to a place of uncertainly when she is emotionally full.

It feels like the waves of the sea brushing up against the outer perimeters of my senses. I am aware of the cosmic activity that stirs within her place of dwellings. When everything is silent, I can tell that she is speaking a language that is unspoken to the hearing of the ear. But I can decode her every unspoken word. I see her eyes glowing in the darkest night as though they are florescent in nature.

She moves with the sound of music; her every step is a concerto playing soothing songs of deliverance.

As I reached for her the structure of her molecules that seem to be ungraspable with my hands. But my mind has captured the whole of her being.

I can identify her very whereabouts anytime anywhere. Only the heart of love can find this special girl. For she begins with a desire, turns into a dream and grows into a reality and I alone can see the invisible girl.

The Invisible Girl.

LET ME

Let me kiss your fear with love and drive them from your heart.

Let me hold you while the sun burns brightly only leaving a legacy of hope.

Let me watch your soul glow with time as it illuminates your trust.

Let me feel your reality as I seek to know you beyond the depths of your appearances.

Let me hold the thing, which you so treasure in this life as you allow me to handle your heart.

Let me see you cry while holding your tears in secret place forever. Treasuring the waters of your identity while locking my eyes upon your every whereabouts.

Let me hold your hand while walking in a heart-to-heart covenant that will las beyond our years here on this earth.

Let me be the one you can always depend upon in both the good and the bad times.

Let me be all that you need to be loved and cared for until we are but a memory.

Let me be the one you feel safe and condiment, leaving your soul feeling secure.

Let me.

Goodnight My Love

Good night my love. I thought about you intently all day long, as my heart raced without limitations, moving at the speed of freedom.

I tried to change the direction of my emotions but they kept gravitating back to you. I tried to erase the trail of my longing, but was powerless in my attempts to forget those feelings that are now imprisoned within the confines of my soul.

I have chased the ghost of your shadow without losing the fire of desire for holding you so close.

My eyes searched for the visible body, needing to possess the oneness of your presences, needing a touch of your approval upon the hands of my wanting.

My dreams are filled with replays of words of hope from which my addiction for more of you increases daily.

Time would not allow me to say what I truly want to say in my world to satisfy my hungry soul from the craving to find the peace I need.

Now that I have said was what was on my mind, I say good night my love.

Goodnight My Love

It's Complicated

I know your situation is complicated. I understand why you are hesitant to move forward because there is so many to consider. I understand that you got obligations to others and that is okay.

I know that your situation involves people who are dear to your heart.

I am willing to work with you through your difficult circumstances. I am willing to make the necessary adjustments to ensure that no one goes without the attention needed to feel your commitment to them has not winged nor decreased in affection.

I too want you to feel protected. I want to hear the comfort of your whispers while you speak with assurance. I too want to feel the touch of your gentle hands upon the surface of my emotions, as I understand your loyalty to the passion that seeps from your world of giving without restriction.

I too want those tender moments to register through the pure spirit as I lay within your arms. I want to be the healing balm you need during time your time of rest. I want to offer you the greatest care as I handle you with urgent and tender care. I want to be by your side when uncertainly creeps in and steals your reality of real love. I want to be your friend you long for in the hours of despair, so you know that I really care.

I want to not only express it with words but also in my silences as you read my eyes. I want to hold that "Pot of gold" your heart in my hands.

As you become more comfortable with trusting another with your most precious gift, yourself. I know that it is complicated, but I still want you and all that comes with it,

It's complicated.

Father

She was an inscription written by the description of her father when He mentioned the dimensions of her spoken existences. She was designed to reside by the Father's side so that He can guide her every step to anticipate those joyful moments of her life, so that they could spend a lifetime together to weather every storm of life, morning, noon or night. Father would never leave nor forsake her in those most difficult episodes of life; you see she was always on the father's mind.

Father neither sleep nor slumber always protecting her from danger seen and unseen. She was Father's dream of fulfilling His desires of walking in power, though she bears scars, scraps, wounds, and a broken heart and disappointed by others.

Father was the key to her healing, deliverance, freeing her from her captivity and revealing all her potentiality that leads to her possibilities that would free a world of others just like herself.

She is truly the beautiful creation Father created long ago in past time. She is forever and always on His mind.

Father.

Bruised Tattoo

She was all tattooed on her face and arms, which told a story like so many times before. But it was plainly seen they were bruised tattoos from her boyfriend who liked to rough play to show and tell the story of his jealousy.

She was beautiful without the blacks, blues, greens, and red color that covered her body like tapestry of colors displays of historical abuse. It seems like it was no use in telling her to leave him because she had become accustomed to being treated as if she was worthless piece of nothing. Like the proverbial frog in a pot of boiling water, she did not recognize that the continual beating could cost her, her life.

As time began to unfold and her body had weakened, it could no longer take the bombardment of blows from the so-called hands of love. Her mind was paralyzed from the lies he told froze her memory for a lifetime. Trauma has taken its toll on the recycling process of her body.

She had become unrecognizable, so she faded from an oblivious stage of being into a vegetative state of existence, not knowing, not caring, and not living the life she was created to be.

She was created to be loved unconditionally, and protected by loving hands, not the hands of her perpetrator.

Bruised tattoos.

When God Says "No"

It is difficult to accept moments of disappointments.

In our lives when we have prayed, but it seems the answer is no. Does everything we pray for is the best option or solution to our dilemma?

However, when we trust in the God of our souls we can have confidence that everything will be all right. Moreover, when it seems like we cannot comprehend or grasp what is going on in our lives will we still have confidences in His ability to guild us through the most difficult situations that may arise.

It is never easy when you believe you are on the right track only to find out that you been missing the marks. I have prayed for things that never manifested only to find out later on the road if I had gotten what I wanted it would have destroyed me. Thank God for His amazing grace and mercy.

When God says "no" He is able to distinguish what is appropriate for our daily lives. There were times that I regret ever praying for certain things in my life because when I got it, I wish I could have given it back, but it was too late.

So, you must be very careful when petitioning the father for things, people and situations. Believe me when God says, "no" He has a good reason for saying it.

When God says "no".

Déjà vu

There are moments in time recognized as a repeat memory from time past you felt you had been here before. There are glimpses of the past that capture your attention for space of time and you say to yourself. "I been there before".

You cannot quite figure out how but deep down inside you know that you know. It is what you call a "Déjà vu". It feels like we lived a past life but not sure why, what when, or where.

The spirit of man is not limited to just this presences time, but it moves beyond time and space because it is the eternal part of our being. We really do not know how powerful we are.

We were created in His (God) imagine and likeness. It is kind of funny how we just know, but do not know how we know.

We have this amazing insight that can be used for good or bad, depending upon the choice you make.

So, the next time you have a "Déjà vu" don't chalk it up as just nothing.

It could be a reminder of something that happened long ago as a reminder that when you have those "Déjà vu' moments of reflection of the past, the present and the future is all connected.

Déjà vu.

The Color Pink

She loves the color pink.

The color pink represents the universal love of oneself and other people.

Her ways are tender and nurturing. Her hands are soft as humanity, as the world needs her gentle loving ways.

The color signifies compassion, understanding, giving, and receiving, unconditional love.

One who loves pink is making a statement that they are friendly and are approachable and very sensitive to condition of others.

Pink is associated with being very polite, non-threating with the essences of optimism and hope.

Her life was laced with the characteristics of being trustworthy and a confidant holding the history of others past in high esteem. She will not betray the loyalties of those who are seeking refuge in the promises heart.

She follows the buoyancies (convictions) of her true calling to heal the nations of conflict and despair.

The color pink.

That Night

The night I shall never forget for it was a night of passionate love. Love is forbidden due to the sensitivity of its nature.

The night was a night when we touched mind, body, and spirit, losing all sense of reality, freed from all restrictions of restraint.

That night I will never forget the look in your eyes as if a whole new world of knowing, seeing, touching, holding feeling had come into the realm of reality.

Knowing as if known, seeing as if seen, believing, and hoping even, hope for the moment of truth. The night shall be a memorial throughout eternity, etched in history, and told by many for years to come. That night will be a night embedded in the unconscious banks of our minds, leaving a trail of wisdom for those who will soon follow that path of intimacy, an act only learned by those who are committed to building strong everlasting relationships forever.

That night.

Poetic Bandit

Poetic bandit, he is smooth with his words, leaving a trait of wanting waiters in line for more of his kind, speaking soft smoothing something that to his subscribers from reality to fantasy to ecstasy, you had better believe what he spoken was not free, but his patrons could not get free due to the addiction of his conviction.

The poetic bandit has been accused of many crimes; some say it was his hypnotic mellow words someone heard through free speech, and now they want him to be impeached because he made promises they say he did not keep, leaving a trail of unattended hearts, who craved for more of his attention, he is known as the poetic bandit because he spoke healing to the broken hearts, he spoke life to the dead lives, he spoke love to the unloved forms of shapes, colors, and sizes of the softer nature, therefore, he became responsible, liable, and accountable for all those that heeded to his therapy, and so now we know the whole story, no need to worry, it's on the Poetic Bandit.

Poetic Bandit

The Beauty of a Broken Heart

The beauty of a broken heart is the tenderness of openness.

The beauty of a broken heart is one that is loving and gentle embracing every moment of happiness—lost through the dark storms of life.

The beauty of a broken heart reveals the very nature of gestures leaving a void of uncertainty, which can be known through fellowship of seeking.

The beauty of a broken heart is the love given that is purified through moments of intimacy that is forever—where the caressing of touching is beyond the imagination Though the heart is dismantled it will give from its very nature and that is to be shared at all times—with the intended to be given from a heart of sharing and caring.

The beauty of a broken heart is the warmth of kindness—the picture of reality the road to success paving a side road for those who lost their way The beauty of a broken heart is the glow of comfort the assurance that no matter how hard things become in life there will always be a place to go where love moves without restrictions, love grows without hindrances, where love knows love and embraces it with open arms—the beauty of a broken heart.

The Beauty of a Broken Heart

First Lady Michelle

*N*ever have I seen a first lady so eloquent, more beautiful than all the queens I have ever walked the earth in human form. Like a dream, she is everything a king could ever hope for. She is full of wisdom and understanding, her truth is sought after by the powers that be. Her gift to humanity could never be replaced with just ordinary, because what she carries in her spirit is the life of the people.

No price could ever be exchanged for the sacrificial price she pays to walk in glory. Her heart is knitted with unconditional love that moves mountains; she is a restorer to the breached soul, wondering without hope.

With her life, she gives beyond human comprehension that comes from supernatural intervention. Gracefully, she stands her ground and smiles when others do not understand the high call upon her destiny to change the course of a nation's perception of real change.

Her ways are stealthy in nature, revolutionary by design, and truthful in originality. Only a first lady with the heart of a visionary would dare to take on feats of impossibility only to stand victorious.

Born with the innate ability to discern the times, she moves with intelligibility and assiduousness to bring deliverance to a broken nation.

Her role as first lady must be one of great character and astuteness. She is a role model for women who desire to walk in a place of power and integrity. An educationalist for those who desire to see a lady in raw form, groom from birth to wear a crest only fitting for a first lady.

First Lady Michelle

Never Have

Never have I found someone so perfect. You, you are the chain to my connection of glowing as one the total sum of love.

Never have I been so engulfed with the spirit of your presence, promising my heart to surrender its commitment to be the sole provider of intimate situations, an occasion for an explosion of something good to take place so I can track you down when I need a refill of your sweet seduction.

Never have I met one with more intention to give more than what was required to satisfy all that is included in the circle is wanting more of heaven's enlightenment.

Never have I needed someone who has influenced my heart to flutter without skipping a beat on the path of continuity, always feeling the comfort of comfort.

Never have

Beautiful, Beautiful

*A*nd she was beautiful, beautiful both inside out, both interior and exterior without a shadow of a doubt. She was about as real as life itself.

I could feel that this was real because I was moved by feelings I started to draw from her spirit.

In my mind, she was my lost-in-found dime piece, and it was just a matter of time before I would reconnect to that, which was destined to come back around in the process of time, as she is beautiful, beautiful.

The queen of queens, the love of love, and the reason why I need her is to see her as mine.

The love of my life is better than fine wine that age with maturity. She is the one that frees me up like a prisoner bound by chains. I was caught in despair until she came around.

I have found my one and only beautiful, beautiful.

Beautiful, Beautiful

Chocolate Dreams

Chocolate dreams you are my everything. Imaginable sweet to meet the demands of craving, saving me from a life of crimes, but I'm addicted to the commands of your wishes for brown candy kisses stealing candy dishes to pay for my habits of needing more.

As I soar into the sugar hills of uncontrollable wills of slipping into the hands of I cannot, I can, ups and downs, your chocolate dreams love take me from heaven to hell, the jail of my slavery, you see no matter what, I'm dammed if I do and dammed if I don't.

Chocolate dreams will not let me be close to partaking of your substances until I wake up from this Illusion, my conclusion of intrusion, colorful confusion mesmerized by living a lie.

Your chocolate dreams keep me so high I can fly like a bird in the sky, and when I come down from the mountaintop, do not stop, and just give me some more of that candy rock.

Chocolate dreams.

Picture Of

*A*nd you are the picture of a thousand words that Reflects the many moods I feel, see, and believe.

I believe in all that you are and more and every time I think about how I feel, I can only contribute to the essence of your presence.

Every time I see you, something goes off in my heart like an explosion of liberty, freeing me to partake of your glory.

You cause so many emotions to surface to the top of my exposure, revealing one true self, becoming vulnerable to every whelm of passionate invitation.

You are the picture of many hand sign of communication, thought, perception, beliefs.

Through gesture only understood by one who has the knowledge to interpret what's is being revealed through motions of physical movement capturing the attention of your captive audience to share the most intimate true inter self-working of the manifestation of the pure love.

You are the perfect picture of life, joy and everything that comes with being complete.

Picture of

Glass Mirror on the Wall

Glass mirror on the wall, who is the greatest of them all?

You had better know who you are. The mirror is simply a reflection of what it sees in proportion to what is revealed.

It can't show anymore or less than the truth, but you better know yourself, because when you look into the mirror you will see all the possibilities or the negatives, freeing you or imprisoning you to a life of bondage.

Glass mirror on the wall who knows the best of all?

You must make the call to change the image that you see or the perception you believe.

It's a matter of choice, so choose to use the power of your voice to change that which you do not desire or dictate that which you harbor in your heart.

Glass mirror on the wall who will rise or who will fall, who will capture the reality of what can be, what can be achieved or what can be conceived through the power of belief.

Glass mirror on the wall.

Forbidden

It was forbidden for her to love outside of the traditions of her culture, but the matters of the heart no one can control.

Her eyes spoke volumes of passionate inclinations imprisoned by cultural bondage and enslavement.

She was bound by the beliefs handed down for centuries through words of strict consequences of punishment for loving someone who is not approved of by family consensus.

Her love was incarcerated and surrounded by those who had no clue that her spirit cried out for liberation, but her freedom had to be expressed within the confines of her own imagination, which she alone had access to.

She must control her eyes from wandering off into the place of unbridle lust because there was no place for love except if it was arranged by patriarch and matriarch of heads of families who believed that tradition took the place of any temporary feeling.

Her desires were so deep that she would dream of freedom where love roams without restrictions of foreplay as she dances upon the bed of innuendos reaching out for the love she so desperately craved for.

She would often pray for a night of wild, unleashed, uninhibited strokes of uncontrollable finger-licking good moments of letting loose of her imagination to appease the bondage of her struggles and to allow her body to experience what it was created for and that is real intimacy.

She lived a double life by marrying someone she did not love but was force to and always living in the fast lane of fantasy and insurrection of contemplation of obeying the laws of her customs. She was forbidden in the eyes and heart of others, but in her own heart she lives as she always wished, so that she might survive the miseries of others beliefs.

Forbidden.

Folly

*I*t was a night of exploration of truth unknown to me.

I have seen places kept secret until the appointed time of revealing.

I felt this engulfing desire of one seeking genuine love without the falsification of pretend. I consented freely without any coercion or outward influence.

I knew to a degree that I was traveling into un-traveled waters to squelch my thirst for curiosity. I dangle in the fires of self-annihilation to taste of the forbidden fruit upon the isolated tree of beauty.

I pulled the dry luscious seed from its roots to understand its beginnings and the content of its nature. I gazed over this fruit with my peripheral vision to verify the origin of its substance.

I was aware of the potential exponential power that lay before me calling out to my vulnerability to ride the winds of uncertain risk-taking adventure that may lead to never never land.

It was the thrill of thrills that drew my attention into a place of possible entrapment of unrestricted passion.

Folly has no boundaries, no conscious, and no regrets for committing the unthinkable when it comes to pleasure.

Folly is like a wild child forbidden to play with fire but is willing to take the chance of being burned but looks beyond the consequences only to pursue their own way. Like an uncontrollable urge to jump into the abyss of blind unlearned knowledge the will to challenge the unsearched lure one's heart into a place of compromise to get unpurified information that can only be revealed through defying the odds the takers to attempt the impossible only to yield unto it dares to chance it all for a one-shot deal.

Truth be told we all have played with the piper who whistled a tune that hypnotized, memorized, and polarized, until our hearts were captured with awestruck vision.

Folly.

I See You In

I see you in so many ways as I continue gaze upon all that is beautiful, all that is wonderful, all that is glorious, all that is awesome, all that is anything and all things.

I see you in my heart as the most important one the mind could ever believe, for you are creation in its mirrored form, a reflect of your very character.

I see you in my eyes as the dream of wonderful images of greatness bestowed upon visions of the continually seeking to understand the many marvelous ways you display every day.

I see you in my hearing, for I can hear angels singing the praise of the one who is magnificent, hearing the voice that command all things to be at peace, the voice that stills the waters of life, the voice that speaks secrets in the hearts of men.

I see you in me, because I act, talk, and speak as though I'm emulating the very traits from which I was created to be, therefore, I am bound to be, to see, to achieve all the possibilities of just being Me, because I'm just like thee.

I see you in.

Between the Lines

There is a language that is not spoken with words but with actions.

I have learned that you must be able to read between the lines. People do not always have the courage to tell you they are not interested in a deep relationship.

They sometimes communicate through unspoken words of not returning phone calls, emails, or even texts. They rather treat you with a "long handle spoon" with very little contact.

When an individual is not concerned with becoming intimate, they void deep conversation. They reveal very little information about themselves as those who want to keep the friendship a friendship and at other times, they just do not want to be bothered.

It is more of a humane way of not hurting people's feelings. However, what is worst is someone telling you they are not interested or you leaving you hanging and guessing.

But there are always signs you just must learn the lingo. Reading between the lines allows one to read between the lines will enable others to discern the feelings of individuals without wasting precious time trying to build a strong bond.

Reading between the lines is a sure way of recognizing the language of love.

Between the lines.

A Letter to…

I am writing this letter to find closure for a willing heart that is open to love, unconditionally.

I am seeking solace in the fact that there might have been an opportunity to have something I have been searching for, for so long.

I thought at last I'd found someone I could truly love as my own, only to come up with too much love to give and no one who is ready to receive.

I am not sure what happened in the translation, but that intimacy was looking for a place of expression in the heart of a transplant recipient.

There is no answer for understanding what has transpired during my time of seeking healing from another.

I wish I could turn back the hands of time and catch the moments of misunderstanding. The will to pursue lost its power to hold on to something special and that was you.

I struggle trying to forget that exists. I tried to erase all the time you made me feel like I was in love. I knew I was falling for someone I only knew for a short period, but it seemed like a lifetime I spent with you.

I am amazed at how in a small amount of time how you changed the way I feel about love. I knew I was in love the moment I was willing to do whatever it took to make you happy. I find it difficult to let you go in my heart. I can only wish and pray that I am released for the power of how you made me feel when I was in your presence.

You will always be special to me. If I said I love you, you made me only prolong my battle to win over my emotions. If I said or done anything to hurt, you or offend you, I now ask for forgiveness.

My only desire and intent were to learn to love you as you should be loved, freely. This is my reasoning for writing this letter that we both can be free to love as we choose.

A letter to…

Goodnight My Love

Good night my love. I thought about you intently all day long, as my heart raced without limitations, moving at the speed of freedom.

I tried to change the direction of my emotions but they kept gravitating back to you. I tried to erase the trail of my longing, but was powerless in my attempts to forget those feelings that are now imprisoned within the confines of my soul.

I have chased the ghost of your shadow without losing the fire of desire for holding you so close. My eyes searched for the visible body, needing to possess the oneness of your presences, needing a touch of your approval upon the hands of my wanting.

My dreams are filled with replays of words of hope from which my addiction for more of you increases daily.

Time would not allow me to say what I truly want to say in my world to satisfy my hungry soul from the craving to find the peace I need.

Now that I have said was what was on my mind, I say good night my love.

Goodnight My Love

Somethings

Somethings should be kept secret at times because they can at times open a "Pandora's Box", more trouble than it's worth.

Sometimes silences is truly golden. It's those times when things are revealed that can kill the thrill of joy in your heart.

Opening one's undisclosed information can be an occasion for conversation not desired, heated flames of fire translate into words of conflicting ambivalence.

Due to the sensitive nature of information that's personal can be quiet unsettling when pressured to say things not intended to please the other party.

It takes two to agree to proceed forward in ant relation bound by a covenant of words joined by consenting entities.

Somethings are best not said leaving no room for future grievances, no misunderstandings, no misinterpretations, no missed signals of not knowing. Something's should and should not be revealed. There's a time and place for everything.

Somethings.

Kingdom Man

She said she was seeking a Kingdom Man only, no other need to apply.

She said she has been in many relationships, but none sufficed the longing in her heart. They were never qualified in the first place. Their qualifications were that they just wanted a trophy wife, someone that looked good on the outside, who was told what to do and what to do when to do it without question.

That would not work for an independent woman. The man she said she was looking for lived by certain principles and was not willing to compromise them at any cost. She also said that he was a man that could be trusted, was not unstable and knew exactly what he wanted.

She said her ideal man was a man that knew how to pray and take his family to church every Sunday and not just send them to church while he sat at home and watched sports all day.

He would be the type of man that is a role model for his children and community. He would be involved his community making things better for everyone else. He would put the needs of his family before any other obligations and that includes church events.

He would always be at home at a decent hour, not in the streets acting like he was a boy instead of a man.

She said she was not interested whether he was a baller with a lot of money. They say, "A fool and his money would soon depart".

She said she did not care if he was the finest looking man in the world because looks would soon fade, but if he was a Godly man who trusted God and lived the life, she was willing to check home out with the hope that his story checked out.

Kingdom man

Before Another Man

Before another man steals your heart let me state my case.

I believe I am more than qualified to be the man you need. I know and understand that you need to feel safe.

Let me be clear there is fear when it comes to protecting the ones I love the most. I am willing to give my life for the cause of keeping you from hurt harm or danger.

I also understand that there is something called "Provisions", do not worry I was raised to take care of my own.

I am not lazy and I rise every morning to ensure that my family will have a place to sleep and eat.

I believe you could also use a man of prayer. When I am not around, I will call on the angels to watch over you and our family. I got 24 hours of protection, so you never need to worry about anything.

These are my qualifications as a man, protector, and provider.

Moreover, if there's anything else you need, let's discuss it before another man steals your heart.

Before Another Man

I Need to Know Before

I need to know before I move on if there is a chance of me loving you because I am not sure what is really on my mind. I took some time to give you hints that I am looking for more, but you have not given me a sign that you are interested or if they are some issues standing in the way. I have been allowing patience to take its place.

I did not want you to rush through the matters of the heart. I am not sure if you have been hurt by someone who has claimed to have loved you and did not. I apologize for any broken trust or the breaking of your heart.

I wanted to cut through the chase and get down to business. I need to know before I turned my desires toward another that there was no sure chance of us coming together and being committed to a loving relationship. I want to make sure I have done everything in my power to see if you were open to something beautiful and that is me loving you unconditionally while my heart is open.

I am willing to work through some difficulties to possess your heart. I want you bad because you make me feel so good. I think about you all the time. However, it seems when I try to suppress memories of you it is but temporary.

In addition, if we never become lovers, I hope we can still be friends. I was not trying to guess what you are feeling or assume that you were not interested. So, I am asking what's on your mind. I want to know so I can make adjustments before I go or stay. I will be waiting for your response.

I need to know before.

LIKE

*L*ike a tree with beautiful leaves so was she, tall and beautiful, she was my shade in the daytime and covered me from the hot burning sun, she was my number one cooler.

I would often lay my body upon her solid frame when I was tired from life's journey. She was always there; she would never go anywhere, always dependable, and always could be found in the place I left her last, at the place of my retreating.

I love to lean upon her strong foundation, which over the years has grown in status and has a proven history of standing under every condition known to nature, and yet she still stands tall today.

And when the winds blew upon her hands would wave as though they were giving praise because they changed colors during the rotation of seasons.

I love to reside by her side after a hard-long day and pray while she silently listens to speak out of the depths of my heart to the universe to free my soul from civilization. She is always there for me. I love her and cannot live without the comfort she provides for me.

Like

Red, Green, and Black

She was amazing with her reddish-brown sandy love-burnt hair as beautiful as the Sun.

I could not help but notice this beautiful creation's birth by the hand of destiny.

I could not help myself from staring at those liquid kaleidoscope mint-favored color eyes caused me to ponder why they were so mind-blowing.

Her vision was laced with a variety of colored greens, almost like being in a dream. Moreover, as they changed colors according to her mood, I was in awe.

I was able to discern several passionate feelings. I could tell from her light green eyes that she was in the mood for giving and sharing love.

I was overwhelmed by the way that she served with grace and her hands felt like tender cloth of silk, smooth and soft.

She wore **black** to conceal the beauty within her soul. She was like a queen out of a fairy tale book, but in reality, I held her with my focus, but for a few tender moments.

I knew there was something deep within the depths of her being destined to be discovered.

When she spoke, her voice was calming like a whisper in the night before bedtime, causing a deep sleep.

When she walked by my side I saw a vision of hope, knowing that day she made a difference in my life. She was more than good-looking but exquisite and charming.

She was mysterious, exciting with a taste of exotic favor in her silhouette.

I will never forget those moments of isolated passion that day.

Red, green, and **black**.

BROKENNESS

I saw as she spoke, and I knew was going to take some time to bring her back to the place of wholeness. As I began to examine her history of love, I discovered that there was a deficiency in affection.

I detected through a heart analysis that there had been a blockage that needed to be repaired. As I father explored, I found that her heart was not working to full capacity and a transplant was in order.

I volunteered to perform the surgery knowing full well that it would be a long process in repairing years of neglect.

As I opened her up, I found scars from abuse. I was confident that I could remove them without complications down the road.

I reconnected some clogged arteries that would not allow her deep red blood love to flow into another's heart.

It was a difficult operation to perform but I was successful. In order for her to make a full recovery, she had to experience real love from someone who really knew how to love her so that she could feel the healing balm of his arms.

I also recommended that he should take her on a long walk and hold her hand so she could feel the safety of his presence.

As her personal physician, I also prescribed kisses every day and plenty of caressing from the love of her life to restore the years of neglect.

Brokenness.

Paper Love

She was like love on paper, and every time I would turn her pages, her face changed. It was living in a world of make-believe, but it was more than a fantasy.

It was a falsity; everything I imagined in my mind came to pass. If I liked how she looked on one page I would turn to another hoping that the next one would be more to my liking.

I had had a choice of many. I could choose from what they were at my beck and call and command.

They Never complained about whether I was happy or not with their photos, they just smiled and always looked happy.

Over time, I became addicted to them all. I just love browsing through the resumes of how they felt and what they liked. Many of them were lonely and did not care about what happened, they wanted momentary pleasure so that they could treasure that experience in their minds.

However, they were dying from a lack of commitment. It did not fit into their schedules. You know that they loved videos and taking pictures in the flesh so that they could catch some on-lookers who were caught up with fixation of their transformation from being clothed to going buck-naked and they did not fake it.

They were for real; even I could feel their longing for some company.

To be left alone on the phone with no one to talk to was a lonely thing for her. She needed to talk about personal things that would cause her dream about how she was going to let it out hang out because she was bold without as conscious.

She was not afraid to say, "Hey you", you want to have a good time tonight, without any commitment". She was willing to do anything; there was no shame in her game, but only lust and desire. She was on fire because she was like love on paper.

Paper Love.

Defiled

She felt so unworthy of love. She did not think she was worth loving because she gave all she had to find love.

She used her body as a pawnshop exchange for temporary favors, which only benefited the recipient of her goods.

Her needs were used to satisfy the pleasures of men so that they could deplete her emotional resources.

Her spirit was empty and void of life, drained by strangers who lusted for a quick fix of their own addictions.

She was passed around so many times that her memory lost count of the pair of hands that handled her fragile little body without the consent of a mature adult but a young female seeking the love of a father.

Her defilement was not self-indulgent but was forced upon her by those who preyed on her inability to express the truth that would expose her perpetrators in her own home and community.

She soon learned ways of darkness that would consume her light. Her brightness of innocence was the only thing that revealed true love until it was taken by blackness.

How can one who has been defiled with unconsecrated hands ever rise from obscurity to find hope by discovering salvation?

Salvation is all accepting of broken defiled victims of circumstances. Unconditional love is her beacon of courage to a life of wholeness.

Defiled.

Estranged

We came to know each other through a season of letting our guards down long enough to be vulnerable. Moreover, once we began to understand one another's identities, we then paused in time, realizing we had stepped into the "no zone".

A place where deep commitment was required before possessing fragile, sensitive, information only given for a prenuptial agreement.

For a moment, I understood a joyous love only rendered to one so trustworthy. I was caught up in a state of mind where we stayed for a time on end.

I was free to reveal my true self without judgmental precepts present to convict me of crimes of passion.

In reality, I was guilty of loving without a state license, but what I felt went beyond, superseded any man-made restrictions. I was bound in the moment of sharing, giving, and receiving of real emotions.

After having known heaven, I then succumbed to my humanity. I then realized I had traveled to the end of the universe where the potential for romance was endless.

I am still processing the process of deep affection affiliated with human interaction.

My heart was exposed to radiation greater than an exploding star wrapped in aluminum foil. My soul has been toiling in past memories of how you took me to a place of indescribable knowledge prescribed for the love of one's life.

Finding my way back to this reality has been one of difficulty, trying to replicate past actions of deliberation would be a miracle of exponential greatness to repeat the traits of love once again.

Estranged

Let Someone Love You

Why don't you let someone love you?

I know that it can be somewhat tough to share your heart after you have been hurt. Difficult to trust after your expectations have been broken.

At times, you seemed so cold as if no one had been knocking on your door with a warm invitation to love you more.

I realize that pain can be hard to escape from a life that can be traced back to a place of despair, where it looked like nobody cared.

I know that fear can hide our emotions from a world of expression.

I could not possibly imagine you not being loved by someone who wanted to be loved.

However, you must allow someone into your secret place where there is no reciprocation of human emotions. You must make a choice to love aging or stay in your prison of isolation.

Let someone love you.

My Virgin

She was my virgin because her thoughts were pure and my hands washed her body. I was acquainted with the most secret part of her. I understood her and I was not estranged to the deep intimated dwelling of her mediation.

Her soul was visible before me and I knew her. There is no one purer than the one I see naked before me.

She was my virgin who called me into the inner chambers of her spirit. She was not afraid to let me see her vulnerability to someone other than herself.

The love she possessed was innocent, never being defiled with foreign hands that were not concentrated. My love is unconditionally available forever.

She will never have to wonder whether my affection will cease to flow through open souls.

I have never known one more deserving than my virgin.

My Virgin

Unwrapped

*L*ike a present being unwrapped, I took my time to dishcloth her unwanted disappointments to replace them with approval. I was careful not to pull or tug too hard because I did not want to take anything vital to her healing.

I want to be the balm that heals from the outside in and from the inside out once, I have moved past the barriers of restriction that would forbid me from entering into the private sector of her life.

I know I need a high-security clearance to behold such sensitive information only privy to the possessor of precious treasure. Before, I touch her, I will consecrate my hands with love so that there will not be any contamination of unwanted intimacy illuminating around as she began to expose her glory to me.

I want to handle her with express care, overnight propriety and ensure her safety with being unwrapped without any damage to the content of her vulnerability.

She needs to know that the hands that hold her tender substances will not crush or squeeze, but she will be pleased with the caressing of her goods. She then needs to know the one who is qualified to uncover her most secret place where she is open to receiving unconditional love with affection.

I know that she is fragile and I must go slowly when touching the surface of her beginning to stop any apprehension of care. As I guild my hands upon her tender soul, she will then know that it is okay. And she will lay there without fear until I'm done with removing all the covering that covers up her beauty.

Unwrapped.

Toxicity

I see the toxicity that can stain the memory if there is not a purging system in place to chase all the negativity away.

I must remove the visions and dreams of others who infiltrated my space of mediation to alleviate its power of persuasion from my imagination.

I feel the poison slowly sipping as it drips from the unrefined lips with no tips on how to take impure knowledge to saturate it with hyssop to increase its potential for good.

Toxic conversation only reveals the lack of truth needed to elevate the mind to a new place and time. To be toxic is to be hazardous to all that are exposed to its content, slowly killing my existence from the life that I need to survive the onslaught of attack upon my humanity.

Toxic relationships are dangerous to those who are seeking to stay healthy. The only way to deal with toxicity is to detox.

Toxicity.

When We

When we agreed to make love, we decided to travel to a place of undisputable pleasures because we were treasures of one another beliefs.

We agreed to venture beyond the secrets and into revelations of each other's world.

We would be privileged to see the glories of kept riches of one another's most prized possessions, our uncontrollable passions.

It takes the beliefs of two lovers who are compatibly matched to experience intimacy on a level that goes beyond one's imagination.

There is a place in love that is strictly for those committed to giving unconditional affection for a lifetime.

When we.

Of Yesterday

The words of yesterday have followed me down through life.

Like a hunter after prey seeking to slay my self-image of possibilities of being great. I heard someone speaking about death many years ago who had a negative flow trying to stop me from moving forward toward my destiny.

It has been a struggle to hold on to my vision, trying not to forget my mission to the land of promise.

The voice of doubt continues to cry, "You can't make it". Nevertheless, I know if I keep my eyes on the prize, I will find the will to yield my hope to all that is good.

There is life and death is in the power of the tongue. As I look back in time, my Naysayers saw something in me that would transform myself, but also others.

I have had to fight the printed assaultive curse spoken from assaultive tongues of indifference and hatred.

I saw my dreams from afar and was not willing to give in to failure without a fight. I have walked through many "valleys of shadows of death" only to rise in victory.

Of yesterday's struggles has been my making of being strong and an overcomer. Yesterday is dead and gone. Today we have and must make the best of it.

Moreover, tomorrow has not arrived yet, but with perseverance, all things become possible.

Of yesterday.

Russian Roulette

There is a danger when it comes to love. There is a time when love can become risky. There is a difference between lust and love.

One is without commitment and the other is buyers be aware. Russian roulette is like gambling with your knowing there is a possibility you may lose. Alternatively, you might call it a lover's addiction.

Some people cannot resist the urge to purge when it comes to having restraints in relationships.

The motto is, you have it your way while you can. All is fair in love and war type of attitude towards others in relationships. Thinking they can have their cake and ice cream too. Only to find out that the one they confessed to love so much has had enough of the dumb stuff and called it quits.

Never play with the heart of another because you just might be the one that gets broken. Most people cannot handle the payback after the tide is turned out of their favor.

It is then too late to say I am sorry for all the years of abuse and misuse. Now they want to be forgiven after flaunting their infidelities everywhere.

What you sow you shall also reap.

It may not be soon, but you had better believe it is going to be later.

It is just a matter of time before you start crying. If you cannot do the time, do not commit the crime of breaking hearts.

Russian roulette.

I Loved Love

If I had never again experienced a touch of a woman I would have been exposed to glory. If I had never held her close again, I would have loved love.

There is something you just know when it comes to love.

It is a feeling so indescribable that it must be shown through actions, not words.

It is an overwhelming experience of understanding that when two people connect it is like an explosion in your soul.

My mind repeats moments of intimate encounters that will not allow me to ever forget the joy you felt while you were together.

Life is never the same after you have tasted heaven right here on earth. My encounters with love were a defining moment that altered my perception of commitment.

I am willing to do whatever is necessary to maintain that state of ecstasy.

There is no sacrifice I am not willing to pay. There is no effort I will not make.

I loved love in a way that made my life complete.

I loved love.

She

She was a she but acted as if she was a he because he defiled her and changed her world.

Her changed into him because he dimmed the light in her life and caught a life sentence of trying to understand the why for his actions.

However, she has accepted the switch roles, so she goes on with her life accepting what happened that night.

She says she is fine but things have not changed with time.

His life is filled with blind rage; her alter ego has taken center stage. Now she parades him in her, it seems like there is a dual personality deep down inside her that has been transformed into him but she is still she.

She.

Tenderness

As the wind of her spirit traveled past the presence of my existence, I discerned that there was something amazing about the way she walked, as though she was graced with stilt movement in every step she took. There was a quietness that saturated the whole of her being, almost like a dream in 3-D.

I could clearly see the true reality of her destiny. She spoke in a gentle proficient manner and the power of her low-tone voice changed the authenticity of my perception.

It was through her unconcealed words that I was able to conceive truth that alluded to my comprehension of her history.

Her eyes were like windowpanes in the fourth dimension revealing revelations only to those who could decipher her purpose for living in the third dimension, the reality of this world.

There was a tenderness that very few possess.

Nevertheless, she was sculpture like a futuristic Mona Lisa arrayed in loveliness, draped by the glory of the Sun.

Even the angels gaze upon her mirror image with envy, and at the time of her creation she was highly favored to be blessed with joy, and as she continues her journal on the path of this life, she bring evolution to the hearts of those that need her most, tenderness.

Tenderness.

Ego

The ego is the I of self, the one that identifies with Self-preservation, the supreme means of seeking to find one's place in a world of lost realization and to define one's purpose of self-actualization wanting to be recognized as a sole entity, wholeness of liberty.

Ego strives to advance the cause of a better exaltation to see all.

Be all, to have all, to know more than the average mundane circumstances that prevail over unsuspecting victims searching for higher elevation.

Egos are the braggers of verification working to be known, to be exposed by coming out of the darkness of hidden agendas.

There is a positive and negative side to the egomaniac of Dr. Jackal and Mr. Hyde showing both the dark and the light side, the good and the bad, and the wickedness and purity of vulnerability.

The ego is a subtle culprit of succeeding or failing, the ego if you feed it, it will grow into something great provided you do it with discipline or starve it and it will become some of the most heinous crimes known to humanity.

The ego possesses the power to harness the greatness of influence accomplished in the world has ever known; it all depends upon what you do with it.

We have control over the development of the ego. The ego will lead you into a life of disparity or a life of possibility.

Ego.

Skel'leton

everybody has skel'letons in the closet of his or her mind. Ghosts from times gone past imaginations of what happened during the hours of gloss sand, slowly slipping from the conscious to unconscious.

Their bones groan with moans of hidden secrecy of some ecstasy and miseries.

Skel'leton from the grave thoughts lay to rest only to come out of the past to reveal the madness of yesterday's folly.

If a polygraph were taken, it would awaken the things unseen by the eyes and mind, flowing through times forgotten fullness, the bliss of darkness.

Skel'leton was often seen as a place where things were dangling around as if a crypt-like clown with so many sad faces and frowns and everybody have a skel'leton.

Just open the closet of your mind and there will be at least one.

Skel'leton.

Medusa

*e*very time men look into the eyes of Medusa, their hearts becomes a little more hardened than before.

She has this hypnotic ability to captivate their eyes for a moment of time while crystalizing their minds to a place frozen in time only to slay them for a lifetime.

She is like a chameleon, changing colors, body shapes and she dances and moves with a persuasive movement of entrapment.

Men are infatuated by her physical appearances like being caught in a trance of romance, but more like curiosity, "Kill the cat", to see how she performs with abilities out of the norms. She a wonder to behold, but her sole goal is to steal their souls.

One must not stare at her quintessence. She is more powerful than the one can imagine. One must be careful when giving their attention to one so beautiful and fair least one becomes enameled in a stone setting.

Medusa

Honeymoon, After-moon, Reality

When two people meet, they become very excited about the possibility of finding someone that is perfect for them.

When the honeymoon starts feelings are at an all-time high, and endorphins flow through the body and mind with good hormones and euphoric thoughts of everlasting love. All is good and everything is perfect.

Honeymoon sparks and then things begin to decline. There seems to be a change of mind, and now as begin to come down off of all the fantasy they start realizing and see all the imperfections to which they begin to say in their minds "Oh boy".

Coming off the highway of heaven they begin to decline into another reality called the "After-moon", feelings are leveling out which are out of control.

They settle down where both can see level ground. The smoke has cleared, and they began to understand certain possibilities and certain work-abilities, and the non-possibilities.

The reality is that the person that you once saw as the greatest thing since homemade slice bread becomes somewhat of a nightmare with thoughts of negativity. It becomes like a chess game, everybody checking one another trying to make the right move, some good, some not good.

They began to ask the tough questions, which for the most part no one answered because everybody wants an impeccable resume. Then we check for and see if there is any computability.

Good looks alone are not enough to build a positive relationship. It takes hard work to understand the opposite partner, friend, and lover. Sometimes fantasy goes from what you thought to what is the naked truth.

Moreover, sometimes we do not like what the truth presences, but we must count the cost before a lonely place to spend one's day hoping for the love of a lifetime.

Honeymoon, after-moon, reality.

Mommy Don't

Mommy don't kill me. I know you are afraid of having a baby out of wedlock, but it's okay, God forgives.

Mommy, I can feel your thoughts and everything you go through. I know that you are stressing, and I am too. However, that is okay; you really need to think about what you are about to do.

I can hear you talking to other people about aborting me. Mommy, if you abort me, you will lose a part of yourself, you will never be able to experience what it is to love someone you carried for nine months.

Mommy it is okay, just take your time before taking a life that is precious.

Mommy, I know that you are young and you feel like you made a mistake, but I am not a mistake and God knew that I was going to be conceived on a particular day and time.

Mommy, if you do what you are going to do, you will regret it for the rest of your life.

Mommy, if you decide to separate us you will wonder for the rest of your life what might have been, grieving for me time you have left here on earth. Mommy, if you take that risk, you may kill the both of us and we may never truly know the love we could have shared between mother and baby.

Mommy Don't.

Unborn plead

There was a plead from the unborn child warning the mother not to separate it from the womb because there would be consequences later on.

I could hear the voice of the fetus crying because it would soon lose its home of protection and love being safe in a better world the womb of the mother.

The child would move back and forth reminding the mother that she has an obligation to preserve her life as well as the life of the unborn child.

Children sense death coming through the nervous system of the mother as she detaches herself from a part of herself that she is willing to cut and tear from her body for the sake of saying I am not ready to have this child.

A voice speaks for itself because it cannot speak for itself except through movement in the mother's stomach. The longer the child stays in the womb the greater the chance for survival.

The instinctively began for it has to feel the mother's fears and lack of concern for its temporary residence in the belly while hearing the poor advice about why she should not keep her unborn child.

Life begins at first sight of blood, but life and others begin to defend her rights to do as she please, but not realizing she had an obligation to protect as well as defend an unborn fetus that can't defend itself accept as a consistent reminder of morning sickness and hunger pains that drive the mother to eat when the child has need.

The question is will this mother heed unto the voice of the child or the voice of murder.

Unborn plead.

Virtuous Woman

She was called a virtuous woman characteristics of her heart were pure in nature. She was flawed just like any other woman but what set her apart from others was her intention to love unconditionally.

The question was who can find one who is strong in moral and mental qualities?

She is perfect morally, trustworthy, invaluable versatile, generous, fearless, respected and so much more.

The virtuous woman has to be found amongst a crowd of women or discovered. She stands out in the crowd as if all of heaven cries out saying, "She's over here".

She is made in the secret places where she is not seen but heard. When she speaks, everybody takes notice for her wisdom reveals revelation knowledge to all that had an ear to hear.

Her family depends upon thrifty insight. Her husband can rely upon her in the most difficult times. All of humanity depends upon a virtuous woman for the wat she lives and perform all of her duties, both to her family and society.

Virtuous woman.

I Went Inside

I went inside of her world and tested all of her experiences to truly understand who she really was.

Once I have had the opportunity to explore the grounds of her dwelling. I could see her reality.

I was exposed to history not revealed to anyone else but that special someone who would not pass judgment. Inside I saw some pain and joy, some light and darkness, and yet I felt obligated to protect and cherish the knowledge I now possess.

There is no turning back nor could I unlearn, unseen, unknown her truth. I had been saturated with her vulnerability.

I then had to make a choice to love her in spite of what I knew. I felt a deep passion for her while yet bearing the scars that have marred her purity. \

However, my love was so deep I was able to handle all the difficulties, she had known in her lifetime.

I went Inside.

So You Feel

So, you feel like a caged animal almost like Hannibal the cannibal. Your rage is unprecedented like nothing I have ever seen.

Instead of living the dream, you are experiencing nightmarish hallucinated video schemes, and you complain about the way things are, but are propagating the diabolical plan by that other man, who got in your mind like a puppet master trying to bring disaster to plaster your thoughts into a lower level of process thinking.

Bringing you to the edge of self-published destruction because you can barely function on an intellectual level of discerning who the real culprit behind the scenes is.

So, you feel like you want to fight everyone who challenges your beliefs, and it is more likely you need some educational debrief.

Your belief system is whacked. Wait a minute before you attack. Being outmanned and outgunned does not look like it's gonna be much fun.

So next time someone older than you try to spit game to change your unfiltered point of view which you have no clue, take a minute, think about and pause, let wisdom and revelation talk, and then you will understand, when you really know then you will truly know, how I really feel.

So, you feel.

Touch

I remember that moment when she gently embraced the palm of my hand; it was an unexpected act of consensual acceptance of her invitation to stand in solidarity.

In that space of time, I read the language of the palm of her hand sending messages of hope and assurance.

I felt the unification of her commitment to build together a sworn oath that would last forever. At that moment when our souls collided, our eyes began to glow with burning fires, which turned into nova's of exploding visions that emerged as one.

The touch is a unique occurrence that only happens once in a lifetime.

We were amazed as our hearts gazed over with a translucent coding of pure love and affection, the protection of our covenant allowing some to see the manifestation, but we only knew the depth of deep intimacy.

We both experienced the indelible marking of our hearts being tattooed together while we both possessed half-and-half of the symbols to verify our destiny to be complete and whole.

It was the touch of infinite unconditional love that will last throughout eternity.

The Touch.

My Secret Lover

In the wee hours of the morning dawn, I hear your tender whispers calling my name as I rose from my bed of slumber.

I caress the soul of your beckoning my presence for a rendezvous I then fall back into a daze as if I was floating between a dream and a vision.

I saw you as though you were more than a figment of my imagination.

I knew from the very moment I laid eyes upon your essence I knew somehow you were mine. And as we engaged into atmospheric communications, I felt the intense longing to be by your side.

I was willing and able to make any sacrifice to keep you by my side.

You are my everything and more than I could ever pray and hoped for. You are my queen, my dream. my everything my secret Lover.

I have waited a lifetime for you just to spend eternity with you. You completed my travels on this journey called life.

Never a day goes without thanking heaven for my blessing.

Your eyes sparkle in the night while we set next the fireplace reflecting your vision. When I touch the palms of your hands liquid love flows through my veins from the healing virtues contained within your spirit.

I have been transformed into another man because you were the hope of my hope, the dream of my dreams, manifesting in this here and now, my secret lover.

My Secret Lover.

Nothing

Nothing is guaranteed in life but what you are able to verify is true.

Everybody's truth ain't your truth, truth be told.

They say documentation is everything. Unsubstantiated stories are simple stories with unauthenticated beliefs without proof.

The proof is in the pudding. If there are 2-3 witnesses' credence, then established as being the

Foundation for further investigation and establishment of reality.

There are two types of being: reality and fantasy.

Sometimes we live in multiple worlds of beliefs and escape falsehoods.

On the other hand, they say that two things are guaranteed in life, and that is death and taxes and that is for sure.

If that being the case, we should take every opportunity to get the most out of life.

Never take life for granted or the opportunities allotted to you. Tomorrow is uncertain! Moreover, even though we cannot predict the future, we can sure enjoy what time life has given us to make the most of it.

Nothing is.

www.ingramcontent.com/pod-product-compliance
Lightning Source LLC
Chambersburg PA
CBHW051600010526
44118CB00023B/2760